I'd Love to But I Have a Game

I'd Love to But I Have a Game

27 YEARS WITHOUT A LIFE

MARV ALBERT
with Rick Reilly

DOUBLEDAY
New York
London
Toronto
Sydney
Auckland

PUBLISHED BY DOUBLEDAY
a division of Bantam Doubleday Dell Publishing Group, Inc.
1540 Broadway, New York, New York 10036

DOUBLEDAY and the portrayal of an anchor with a dolphin
are trademarks of Doubleday, a division of
Bantam Doubleday Dell Publishing Group, Inc.

Library of Congress Cataloging-in-Publication Data

Albert, Marv.
I'd love to but I have a game : 27 years without a life / Marv Albert with Rick Reilly.
    p.   cm.
1. Albert, Marv.   2. Sportscasters—United States—Biography.
I. Reilly, Rick.   II. Title.
GV742.A52A3   1993
070.4′49796′092—dc20
[B]   93-4587
CIP

ISBN 0-385-42024-2

10   9   8   7   6   5   4   3   2   1

To Max, who gave me my first reel-to-reel tape recorder, and arranged for convenient installment payments.

—M.A.

To Kellen, Jake and Rae, who make it very hard to go into the den.

—R.R.

Acknowledgments

The authors, while offering no actual monetary thanks, would nevertheless like to express their heartfelt gratitude to David Letterman, David Gernert, Amy Williams, Richard Lewis, Art Kaminsky, Al McGuire, Marty Glickman, Evan Bell, Dick Ebersol, Terry O'Neil, Bob Gutkowski, Mike Weisman, Bucky Waters, Bob Costas (twice), Dave Katz and his crack staff, Robert Klein, Ed (Rim Shot) Markey, George Carlin, Jerry Seinfeld, Al Albert, Steve Albert, Max Albert, Linda Reilly, Janet Pawson, the remarkable H. Howitt, whoever it is that makes the great coffee at the Caesar's coffee shop, Kevin Monaghan and his Ring record book, Bob Morton, Howie (the Electronic Wizard) Singer, the long-suffering John Andariese, Sal (Red Light) Messina, Rob Burnett and his cracked staff, Dr. Frank Field, Ed Maull, Scott Tucker of Caesar's, John Cirillo, Pat Riley, Paul Maguire, Ahmad Rashad, Maury Povich, Tom Brokaw, Sen. Bill Bradley, Mr. Stats Himself Elliot Kalb, David Stern, Al Michaels, Bill Parcells, Linda Chico, the superb Garden photographer George Kalinsky, Barry Watkins, Mike McCarthy, Tommy Roy, Andy Rosenberg and the boys, Dave Jennings, Phil Mushnick, David Neal, who now has voting rights in Seoul, and especially to the late Mike Cohen, who is undoubtedly shaking his head and grumbling, "If this book is going to work, you better get *plenty* of ink." And, of course, the Czar of the TeleStrator, now the renowned Czar of Cleveland, who meant so much to us during his three years of NBA color commentary on NBC.

Contents

Introduction
by David Letterman

For the last twelve years I have happily spent every free minute of my personal life traveling the width and breadth of this great land of ours, literally crisscrossing the United States dozens of times. Driving from small town to small town, addressing church and civic groups, performing at county fairs, judging fishing derbies, entertaining at roadside carnivals or simply dropping in on Mr. and Mrs. "Front Porch" for the sole purpose of lightening the load, brightening the day, putting a smile on the face of a weary twentieth-century America. My appearances are always quite well received and feature a charming mix of true-life stories, poems, inspirational skits, character dance, health pointers and plenty of what I call "good old-fashioned laughter." Plus, you never know when you just might learn a thing or two. The one thing that I have learned from the personal odyssey of joy is that in these crazy times of high-tech computer razzle-dazzle and chilling media reports of radioactive facial tissue, most people are still pretty darn nice if you give them half a chance. As I visit with folks at the various gatherings, performances, spiritual chats or individual counselings, the one question I'm asked time and time again is "Dave" ("Mr. Letterman" if it's a church or youth group), "is it true that you went to Mexico to have some kind of secret surgery?" Well, I always handle this question the same way. I take a nice long sip of my special "public-speaking punch," clear my throat, wipe my mouth and holler back, "If I did, I sure as hell wouldn't tell you." Man, does that ever bring down the house. I guess the reason people seem to enjoy that particular remark so much is that I always put a little fake chuckle in my voice when I deliver it, which I think helps folks understand there are no hard feelings. Whatever the reason, it really is foolproof, and if you find yourself called upon to do a little public speaking, please be my guest and give it a try. I've also found that once you snap off a zinger like that, it discourages show-off punks who enjoy turning positive uplifting experiences into something ugly. The other comment I get quite a lot is "How long have you known Marv Albert?" I have a pretty good comeback for this one also. I use my real high girlie voice and I say, "Oh, you mean the sports blooper boy?" Well, when they hear that, they want me to run for President or something. I first met Marv Albert in the summer of 1968. I was on the road then too, driving across Texas in my stepbrother Dwayne's '66 big-bore, full-blown hemi-'Cuda. Let me tell you something about that car. It was fast. Working for three years at the Del Rio Dairy Queen, I had saved enough money to put in racing cams, high-torque flywheel and NASCAR rear end. I also beefed up the suspension and added carbon fiber discs all around that pulled close to three g's when you jumped on the binders. By the way, the reason I spent so much of my money on Dwayne's car is that Dwayne suffered from a proprioception disorder which caused him serious spatial disorientation. Obviously he was never able to safely drive a car. Nor, I must say, was he ever really comfortable riding in a car. And to this day I don't believe he has flown. So my point is, in actual purpose, it was my car. That Tuesday afternoon, motoring along state road 183 south of Austin, I caught my first glimpse of Marv Albert. He was standing at the side of the road, in one of his trademark eight-dollar suits, with his thumb out. On a hunch, I wrestled the 'Cuda down to subsonic speed, tossed up a choking cloud of hot Texas gravel and gave him a lift. It was the smartest move I ever made. As we ate mile after mile of two-lane, Marv told me all about himself. Setting fire to his parents' house when he was six. How he planned and botched his own kidnapping. The Tupamaros. Killing a guy.

His early marriage to Kim Novak, and prison. He had a real gift for filling the hours with sparkling conversation. My first impression of Marv? He could not have been more personable. Almost from the beginning, Marv and I became fast friends. I did the driving; Marv took care of the food. Whenever we got hungry, I'd pull off the main road and roll us into some tiny little smudge of a Texas town like Sanderson, Dryden or Pumpville looking for groceries. While I was out front watching the locals enjoy the heat coming off the hood, Marv would sneak into the store and quickly reappear with a shirtful of Kraft macaroni-and-cheese dinners. Not the tall skinny boxes, the deluxe ones that come with their own cans of cheese. Marv and I would dine like kings. For the next five years it was me, Marv and the road. We'd never stay in one place too long. Maybe take an odd job here and there to raise money for rocket fuel and then it was back out on the long black lonesome. The miles, the hours, the days, the weeks all became one long dream. Somewhere in Idaho, Marv helped himself to a harmonica and learned to play Amazing Grace. Let me tell you something, Marv could blow that harp. I'd be lying if I told you we didn't have some tough times. And yes, it's true, every now and then we'd have to check into the old Gray Bar Hotel. Nothing serious. Mostly loitering, public nuisance, rock fights, that sort of thing. Next time you see Marv, ask him why he still can't make a fist with his left hand. Yes sir, we were living and we knew it. We also knew it couldn't last. I can't remember now why it happened, probably a woman, maybe whiskey. Could have been both. But eight miles west of Cedar City, Utah, Marv and I called it quits. Were we hippies? I don't know. Were we drifters? I guess. Were we outlaws? Could be. Were we happy? Never more so.

Well, there you have it. I've told you my story, now let Marv tell you his.

Author's Preface

NO JOB FOR A GROWN-UP

I am loathe to admit it, but my Knicks broadcast partner, John Andariese, thought of the title for this book. People invite me to dinner and I always have to tell them, "I'd love to but I have a game."

"When can you, then?" they ask.

"How about some night in August?" I say.

It's true. Start in September. During the fall, I do one football game a week on NBC. I have to get to the game city Friday to interview coaches and players, to memorize rosters and to start working on the charts I'll use in the booth. That leaves me Monday through Thursday. Monday through Thursday I do the New York Knicks basketball games for Madison Square Garden Network, home and away. Been doing that for twenty-seven years. If for some bizarre reason, there is a day left between Monday through Thursday when the Knicks are not playing, then I do New York Rangers hockey games, home and away. Admittedly, I do not get to many of the road games, but if the schedule permits, I am there with my color man, Sal (Red Light) Messina. I've been doing Rangers games for twenty-eight years. Can't give *them* up. What if they suddenly win the Stanley Cup?

Now, *if,* somehow, all the planets align and I'm not doing an NBC football game or a Knicks game or a Rangers game or catching a red-eye between any of them, and I'm just about to put my feet up on the couch and watch a movie, that's when *Late Night with David Letterman* will call and say that Father Guido Sarducci canceled and would I mind dropping by with a few bloopers.

Some years have been worse. I used to do the Knicks games and the Rangers games along with anchoring the 6 and 11 o'clock sports on WNBC-TV, plus the occasional visit on *Live at Five*. That meant getting up, going down to my office, preparing the pre-game show for the Knicks or Rangers broadcast, doing any interviewing or voice-overs I had to do, then running down to the station, writing and preparing the 6 o'clock sports report, presenting the 6 o'clock sports report, finishing up at 6:30 to 6:45, dashing over to Madison Square Garden, doing the pre-game show at 7, broadcasting the game at 7:30, finishing at about 10:15, driving madly back to the station, writing the 11 o'clock sports with help from crack sports producer Dave Katz and preparing the video, doing the 11 o'clock sports, finishing at 11:30, having my coronary and going to bed.

(It's not like I had a life in childhood either, come to think of it. As a kid, I worked for the Brooklyn Dodgers as an office boy and the New York Knicks as a ball boy while going to school. I was also president of the New York Knicks fan club, kept stats for the Knicks' announcer, Marty Glickman, put out a weekly newsletter, "Knick Knacks" ran my own fictitious, non-air radio station in which I announced into my tape recorder as many high school games as I could get to, plus all the Dodgers games, plus whatever game might be on TV, plus whatever games I felt like re-creating out of the box score in the newspaper, not to mention being sports editor of the school yearbook and writing a monthly sports column called "Right Angles" for the school newspaper, *The Lincoln Log,* plus working as a stringer at high school basketball and football games for the major New York dailies while I was in high school. I was not normal.)

Anyway, as soon as the football season is over, I begin broadcasting a Sunday NBA game on NBC with my color analyst, Mike (the Czar of the Telestrator) Fratello. We usually arrive at the site on Friday. That leaves, again, Monday through Thursday. Same thing applies. Knicks home and away. Rangers on any off nights. Planets align. Letterman.

Now, the last game of the NBA season is usually in the third week of June. I have to unpack, don't I? That pretty much brings us to July. In July 1992, I was in Barcelona, doing the Dream Team games at the Olympics, not to mention the Tournament of the Americas in Portland, Oregon, which came before it, not to mention the week they spent in Monaco. I was done in Barcelona August 10, but I needed to spend a week visiting my son, Brian, attending school in Israel. I finally got home August 18. That left two weeks until the opening of the NFL season, but one of those weeks I needed to do a non-broadcast practice game since I was breaking in a new partner, former New York Giants coach Bill Parcells. So that leaves me one week. I need at least a five-day vacation somewhere, don't I? So that leaves two days, one of which I need to do my laundry. That leaves me *one* night in August.

So where shall we eat?

—MARV ALBERT

*I'd Love to
But I Have
a Game*

Like Marv, I grew up in New York, so baseball has always been my favorite sport. I prefer the fat umpires. I feel if you're on the field and not in the game, you should be in the worst physical condition a human being can possibly be in. That way, it accentuates the athletic ability of the players. Umpires should be allowed to eat *during* the game. Their minds are on their next meal anyway. Wouldn't you like to see an umpire with a big mouthful go, "I think he was out. I'm not sure. The roll was covering part of the base."

—JERRY SEINFELD

1

Fried Rice

I once asked David Letterman to share with our NBC baseball pre-game show audience his favorite baseball memory. He thought about it for a moment and then said, "I'd have to say the time I followed José Pagán home from the ballpark."

As things turned out, Letterman had a lot of touching moments he wanted to share with us about baseball. "Ever since I became a baseball fan years ago, I've had one dream," he told us. "And that's to go to any major league ballpark, have eight or nine beers and then, maybe early in the second half of a doubleheader, jump onto the field and interfere with a ball in play." Naturally, that was a very tender moment for all of us.

He also shared with us the time he went to see a game at Anaheim Stadium. "The Angels were playing the Brewers," he said. "Nolan Ryan was pitching. Unfortunately, I needed to leave early to get back to Los Angeles for a dinner appointment. I got into my car, and I was in such a hurry that I threw the car into reverse without looking. I backed out of this very confined parking space and, just then, I heard a big thump. *Tha-thump!* Like that. Clearly, I'd hit something. I thought, Oh, what could I have hit? So I went back and fished something out of my rear wheels and it was Gene Autry."

During the writers' strike a few years back (which forced Letterman off the air for months), I invited Dave to conduct an interview for our NBC baseball pre-game show, just to keep his interviewing technique sharp. For his interview subject, we chose pitcher David Cone, who was then with the New York Mets. Herewith the text of that historic get-together:

LETTERMAN: I thought, what'd I do is, I made the notes here. We'll just do a dummy interview. [Pause.] Now, as a boy, growing up . . . You did grow up as a boy, didn't you?

CONE: Yes, I did.

LETTERMAN: Did you have dreams of becoming a major league pitcher?

CONE: Yes. Since the day I could pick up a wiffleball bat.

LETTERMAN: You did, didn't you?

CONE: Yes, I did.

LETTERMAN: You and I have something in common. You grew up in Kansas City. I grew up in Indianapolis. Yet we both have something in common. Do you know what that is?

CONE: No, what is it?

LETTERMAN: When we work, we both wear a cup.

Yes, ladies and gentlemen, television for the whole family. As things turned out, baseball was a very fertile subject for Letterman. For instance, we asked him if he had any ideas for the baseball commissioner on how to improve the game. "I think fans should have easy access to the team bus," he said. "Kind of go through their personal belongings while they're out there playing. That would be something that would enhance the enjoyment of the game for me."

Fortunately, my memories of baseball as a kid involve almost no felonies. I was actually *working* in baseball at age 14. I landed a job with the Brooklyn Dodgers through, believe it or not, Howard Cosell, on the ABC Radio Network. I was one of the teenage panelists on one of Cosell's earliest ventures into broadcasting—a program called *All-League Clubhouse.* He'd have a panel of youngsters ask questions of a weekly sports guest. I was a regular member of the panel, which one week featured Dodgers vice president Fresco Thompson as the guest. After the show, I sidled up to him and slipped him my card and asked if he knew of any jobs in baseball for a kid desperate to start working in sports. It just so happened, he had a summer job for me.

Suddenly, there I was, a skinny and shy kid, working daily with the Boys of Summer—Jackie Robinson, Pee Wee Reese, Roy Campanella, Gil Hodges, Junior Gilliam, Carl Erskine, Don Newcombe, Preacher Rowe, Carl Furillo, Walter Alston, all of them. I worked mostly in the ticket office and the mail room, mailing out Dodger schedules, filling ticket requests, running the switchboard once in a while. One of my switchboarding highlights was accidentally disconnecting Walter O'Malley on a long-distance call.

One of my jobs for the Dodgers, looking back on it, was very strange. The Dodgers had a manual scoreboard on top of their office building in downtown Brooklyn and they'd post the score each inning up there so people in town could see it. That was my job. I'd go up to the top floor of the building, shimmy through a crawl space, squeeze through a crevice and get on top of the roof. I'd stand up on the roof and listen to Vin Scully's call of the game on the radio. Each inning, I'd put up the new score. One day, though, I had to put up the wrong score because I couldn't find the "7." I probably cost some poor bookie thousands of dollars.

Alas, all good things must come to an end. Just before the Dodgers announced their move to L.A., I was sent a "Dear Marv" letter, the same letter everybody in the organization received. Mr. O'Malley was offering everybody the same job in Los Angeles that they had in Brooklyn. That was a difficult career choice for me, continuing eighth grade at PS 225 or embarking on a West Coast baseball career. Finally, I was able to come to a decision. My mom said no.

I'd Love to But I Have a Game

Actually, my very first sports announcing job was in baseball. I was the second man in the booth doing the minor league Syracuse Chiefs games—live broadcasts when the team played at home and re-creations off the sports wire when they were on the road. The No. 1 broadcaster was Carl Eilenberg, who happens to be the current mayor of Rome, New York. The details of the games came in pitch by pitch over the wire and we used sound effects and records and whatever we could think of to try to make it sound real. One Sunday afternoon, when Carl was doing the second inning, I wandered away briefly. When I came back just a few minutes later, I was slightly surprised to find Carl doing the *fifth* inning. Somehow, he had skipped the third and fourth innings. He wasn't keeping a careful scorecard and all of a sudden there we were, in the fifth. We just carried on like absolutely nothing was the matter. Those innings are lost to history now, floating around in some weird doubleheader in the Twilight Zone. And do you know what the saddest thing was? Not one person called.

When things go wrong in network television, just the opposite happens. *Everybody on earth* calls. One day, I was scheduled to interview Boston Red Sox star Jim Rice for the NBC baseball pre-game show. At the time, Rice was having his problems with the Boston media, the fans and Red Sox manager Joe Morgan. A couple of games before, he'd hit a key home run and refused to answer the crowd's pleas for a curtain call. Rice had become a bit of a recluse. He didn't do many interviews. Why he did my interview I still don't know. He must have wanted the national exposure. Since I had such a short amount of time, I could only ask one light question before I got into some tougher questions regarding his recent controversies. Then I asked him the biggie: Why didn't he come out for a curtain call the other night?

His face dropped. He stared at me. "You're just trying to make me look bad on national TV," he said.

"No, I'm not," I said. "These are just routine questions that baseball fans are interested in."

Rice grumbled. It was clear the remainder of the interview wasn't exactly happy talk.

That spat between us wouldn't die most of that season. I really wasn't trying to make him look bad on TV. Asking why he didn't acknowledge the fans is not necessarily a negative question. For instance, he could have used it to explain his side of the story. He might have said, "Look, if the fans are only going to cheer for me when I hit a home run and boo the rest of the time, I don't think I owe them anything." But he didn't and I'm not surprised. Many baseball players, more so than other athletes, are pampered. In many cases, they're used to soft questions on the local pre-game shows because those shows are usually controlled by the ball clubs. The questions are puffballs.

The other problem is that there's a game nearly every day. Something is bound to go wrong between the players and the media. You can walk into almost any clubhouse in the country and there will be four or five different players who aren't talking to the local newspaper beat writers. That's because the beat writers *have* to ask the tough questions and they have to ask them practically every day. Let me tell you, you don't want a baseball beat writer's job. Ron Davis, the former Minnesota Twins pitcher, once criticized management for trading away some of the team's top players. When it came out in the next day's newspaper, Davis was fuming. "All I said was that the trades were stupid and dumb," Davis complained. "And they took that and blew it all out of proportion!"

Not all ballplayers will hide from a tough question. After Oakland A's reliever Dennis Eckersley gave up that huge home run to the Dodgers' Kirk Gibson in the World Series a few years back, I had to ask him about it, point-blank, in the clubhouse afterward. He came right on with me and talked about it. No problem. And when I was done, he sat and talked with the writers about it for an hour. Many players would have been soaking in a tub at home by then.

Then there was my infamous Whitey Herzog interview. Whitey, then managing in St. Louis, was considered to be a long-shot candidate for the National League presidency, along with the late Bart Giamatti, who was the president of Yale at the time. The Cardinals had been doing poorly and I ended the segment by saying, "Look at it this way, Whitey. If you don't get the job—as president of the National League—there's an opening for you at Yale."

He stared at me for a moment like I'd just stuck my elbow in his soup. Then he said, "Now you're trying to be funny, Marv. I don't think that's funny." End of interview. I closed by saying, sheepishly, "I guess Whitey won't be appearing on the baseball pre-game show anymore."

All I can guess is that Whitey misunderstood. He must have felt that I was trying to embarrass him, which I was not. I was trying for a humorous transition to end the interview. I mean, how many guys are going to have the qualifications to be the president of Yale University? I know I'm not. I could've used that line on anybody. It was nothing personal toward Herzog. It didn't matter. That became the Interview That Wouldn't Die.

What's surprising is that I never had any on-air rhubarbs with Reggie Jackson. He's changed since his retirement, but I always found him one of the most difficult players to deal with. I've interviewed Reggie dozens of times, since I used to do Mets and Yankees pre- and post-game shows. Reggie was a great player, but he could be one of the most manipulative people I've ever known. You'd ask him a tough question and his answer would always be "All I care about is God and family." Except that when you got to know Reggie, that seemed a little hard to swallow. For one thing, Reggie cared quite a bit about Reggie. This is the man who once marveled at "the magnitude of me." This is the man who said he was "the straw that stirs the drink."

Reggie had a reputation of doing interviews only with guys who would fawn over him. He may have changed by now, but in those days he had a size XXL ego. One time, Gene Wojciechowski of the Los Angeles *Times* poked fun at Reggie's mangling of a line drive in a game by writing, "The only way Reggie will ever win a Gold Glove is by spray-painting one." It was a takeoff of a quote Reggie himself had delivered, yet the next day Reggie lit into Wojciechowski during batting practice. Between and through every swing, Reggie colored the air blue with invectives. Wojciechowski stood there and took it, but Reggie didn't let up.

This went on for two days, until finally Wojciechowski approached Reggie and said, "Look, why don't we get this thing over with. Let's forgive and forget."

To which Reggie said, "Well, Reggie the man can forgive you. But Reggie the ballplayer can't."

Pleeeeeeeease.

Which reminds me of the time infielder (and later manager) Jim Fregosi blew a ground ball that cost his Texas Rangers a game. Randy Galloway, the columnist for the Dallas *Morning News,* wrote that the difference between a Rangers win and a loss that night was "Fregosi's inability to field a routine grounder." The next day, Fregosi was steamed. He sent a batboy to bring Galloway back to the dugout. Galloway came as ordered. Fregosi was smoking a cigarette in the dugout, looking hot around the collar.

"Sit down!" Fregosi roared.

Galloway sat down.

"I just want you to know one goddamned thing," Fregosi said.

Galloway braced himself.

"And that one thing is: No ground ball hit to me is *ever* routine."

Aside from Fregosi, baseball players are among the most sensitive athletes you can deal with. In football, when a play fails or a man scores the winning touchdown, it's not easy to know who screwed up. Was it the tackle missing the block or the safety picking up the wrong receiver? But in baseball, blame is easily assessed. That makes for not only sensitive athletes but some great television moments. That's why, whenever NBC covered the playoffs, I preferred to interview the losing team. The stories are usually better there. The answers are usually better. What you get in the winners' clubhouse is "We're the greatest! He's the greatest! Everybody on this team is one big, happy family!" Then, a week later, half of them have filed for free agency. The 1992 world champion Toronto Blue Jays lost nine players to free agency the next year. But in the losing clubhouse, you get more emotion, you get some upset people and blame occasionally gets parceled out.

I'd Love to But I Have a Game

And yet my most memorable post-game interview came when the losers' clubhouse suddenly turned into the winners'. It was Game 6 of the 1986 World Series between the Boston Red Sox and the Mets. I'd been in the Mets' dugout the entire 10th inning, ready to talk to the apparent losers. The Mets were down by two runs. With two outs, in fact, some of the Mets weren't even waiting for the third out. Keith Hernandez had already gone back to sit in manager Davey Johnson's office to take off his shoes and relax. Kevin Mitchell was back in the clubhouse too, getting ready to shower. But then, incredibly, the Mets came back.

Hernandez had to run back out. A naked Kevin Mitchell had to get dressed again. In fact, Mitchell was in such a hurry he put on his uniform without any underwear. He got a pinch-hit single and scored the tying run. (This is easily the best underwear story we have in the whole book, folks.) Now there's an easy ground ball hit by Mookie Wilson to the Red Sox first baseman, Bill Buckner. Looks like the third out. End of Series. Inexplicably, though, the ball goes through Buckner's legs. The winning run scores.

Suddenly, instead of the losers, I had the flabbergasted winners. Ray Knight, the Mets' third baseman, scored the winning run, so I had him by my side, ready to interview him. Shea Stadium was about to split in half with all the noise and Ray's wife, golfer Nancy Lopez, was crying on his other shoulder. It was madness. And just before we went on, he said to me, quite desperately, "Hold me up. I think I'm going to faint." He wasn't kidding. He was overcome by fatigue and emotion. I could feel him leaning all his weight on me, like he might go any second. So I did. I held him up as we talked. It is the only time in my broadcasting history when I've had to work with a semiconscious person.

Not counting Paul Maguire, of course.

People are always coming up to me and asking, "What's Marv like?" and "How much does Marv make?"

And I always say, "Dad, I don't know."

—STEVE ALBERT

2

Take That,
Mrs. Lipowsky

Everything I have I owe to my sneeze.

I can sneeze on command. I can sneeze anytime I want and make it sound like if I don't get some aspirin and some chicken soup fast, I might die. I can sneeze consecutively, twenty times in a row if need be. My mom used to fall for it every time. Six or seven bad sneezes in a row at breakfast and she'd insist I stay home from school. Now I was free to sit up in my room and listen to the ball games on the radio. After that, I'd play my dice baseball games and announce them into my tape player. I was sick all right.

All I wanted to do then was all I want to do now—be at every game, announce every basket, keep track of every point. I grew up in Manhattan Beach, Brooklyn, the oldest of three brothers and the son of a Hungarian-American grocery store owner, Max Aufrichtig (pronounced Alf-frik-tig). My father tried to get us to work at the store—pricing items, selling comic books out front—

but that wasn't what any of the three of us wanted to do. We all wanted to be broadcasters and nobody on the planet wanted to be one more than me.

Most kids had pictures of athletes taped to their bedroom walls. I had signed photos of announcers and autographs of sportswriters. Some kids made crank calls for laughs. I'd call major league ballplayers at their hotels and leave urgent messages to have them call me. Then I'd interview them for *The Lincoln Log*. Of course, sometimes I wouldn't have anywhere at all to use the interviews, I just wanted the practice. I guess I was a nervy kid when it came to my obsession. One time, Stan Musial returned my call to our house. Our house! My mom, who knew nothing about sports, answered, and apparently it was hard to tell who was more confused, Musial or my mom. Musial thought a Mr. Marv Albert was his New York stockbroker. Mom thought Musial was a catalog salesman.

No matter what sport was going outside our house, I'd either be playing in it and announcing as I played or be up in the "press box"—which is to say I'd open our bedroom window overlooking the action on Kensington Street and call the game from there into the reel-to-reel tape deck my dad bought me. *From high atop Kensington skyline, this is Marv . . .* At night, I'd sit in the living room and try to pick up the voice of the Montreal Canadiens, the late Danny Gallivan, on my shortwave radio. I must have driven my parents insane. I was constantly moving that big old radio around in the living room, trying to find the best reception. I could get Jack Buck in St. Louis, doing the Cardinals games, or on a rare night Jack Brickhouse from Chicago. And when the games were over, I'd study the autographs I'd gotten from sportswriters such as Dick Young or Milton Gross or Leonard Koppett and imagine what they'd write in their stories the next day. Most kids dreamed of going to the moon or being president. I dreamed of running down the third-quarter stats on WHN radio.

By the fifth grade, I probably had more "on air" experience than some guys already in the business. Our teacher assigned us to put on a news broadcast and I was the only one to memorize the script so I could maintain eye contact. I almost walked off the set, though. No TelePrompTer.

When I was in the third grade at PS 195, my teacher, Mrs. Lipowsky, had us write an essay on what we wanted to be when we grew up. I said I wanted to be the broadcaster for the New York Knicks and the New York Rangers. She wrote on the paper that it was "farfetched and unrealistic." Years later, she sent me a note, congratulating me. I still have the paper.

By the time I was in the eighth grade, I had my own imaginary radio station, WMPA (Marv Philip Albert), complete with commercials, interviews, sports updates and game coverage. I would do all the high school games around, plus the Dodgers games and whatever else I could re-create out of the morning box scores. Let's face it. I was not well.

I'm sure my mother was heartsick. She wanted me to make something respectable of myself. She'd take me to tap-dancing lessons, accordion lessons, ballet concerts. Nothing took. I played a lot of piano, but my fingers itched to be wrapped around a desktop mike instead. Ten years I played and all I know is the opening bars to "Malagueña." Brooklyn recital fans still know me today for my rendition of "Malagueña." "Stirring" is the word I believe the New York *Times* used. The accordion I would rather not mention. You know the definition of the word "gentleman"? It's a man who can play the accordion and doesn't.

As an office boy for the Brooklyn Dodgers, a job I procured through Dodgers vice president Fresco Thompson, I was allowed into the press box every game free. Naturally, I *had* to do the games. I'd lug my huge reel-to-reel down to the park on the subway. I'd sit in the club employee section on the other side of a partition from Walter O'Malley himself, owner of the Dodgers, and do the games *exactly* as if I were on the air. I was right next to the booth where Vin Scully was broadcasting. Unfortunately, Mr. O'Malley let it be known that I was disturbing his guests and made me move into a photographer's overhang down the right-field line. I don't think Scully missed me, either.

As if appearing on Cosell's show and working for the Dodgers wasn't enough, I then wormed my way into a job as a Knicks ball

Visiting my father at Fort Bragg Army Base in North Carolina. That's my mother, Alida. *Courtesy of Marv Albert*

As a Knicks ballboy, I rubbed shoulders with NBA stars like Syracuse Nationals' player/coach Paul Seymour. *Courtesy of Marv Albert*

Senator-to-be Bill Bradley signs with the Knicks. © *George Kalinsky*

At one point, WNBC-TV had three Alberts on the payroll at once. On the left is Steve and on the right is Al, who had yet to be issued pinstripes. © *National Broadcasting Company, Inc.*

Dr. J. was not ready for my incredible cross-over dribble. © *National Broadcasting Company, Inc.*

Dr. Ferdie Pacheco receives some much-needed feedback. © *National Broadcasting Company, Inc.*

Joe Namath was among my favorite NBC broadcasting partners.
Incredibly, the football is regulation size. © *National Broadcasting
Company, Inc.*

On the *Sesame Street* set with Gordon, Oscar and Grundgetta. Later,
the tension between Oscar and me resulted in fisticuffs. © *National
Broadcasting Company, Inc.*

From the short-lived Saturday morning cartoon *Pro Stars*. When it went off the air, Paul Maguire was inconsolable. © *1990 DIC Animation City, Inc.*

The night the engineer didn't show up for a Rangers game. Sal (Red Light) Messina and I had to do most of the broadcast by phone. After two hours of talking to Sal on the phone, I went home and crossed him off my "Friends and Family" list. © *Bruce Bennett Studios/New York Rangers*

Surrounded by the finalists of the Marv Albert sound-alike contest.
That's the winner, Barry Lefkowitz, on the right, but they were *all*
very good. I've retained most of them to make annoying calls to
Mike Fratello. © *George Kalinsky*

The night Johnny Carson got desperate for guests. © *National
Broadcasting Company, Inc.*

boy. I think I was picked because I was president of the Jim Baechtold Fan Club, one of the largest . . . *What? You never heard of Jim Baechtold!?!?* Jim Baechtold was a very underrated player. He owned one of the first really classy jump shots in the NBA. He played for the Baltimore Bullets for a year before he came to the Knicks in 1953. He averaged 13.9 points a game one year. What do you want? We, his devoted faithful, put out the monthly "Baechtold Bulletin" (featuring the notes section "Baechtold Bombs") to more than 200 members. He even wrote a monthly column for us. ("The Pivot Foot: Friend or Foe?") Alas, he lasted only five years in the league. He wound up as the basketball coach at Eastern Kentucky. Still can't believe he's not in the Hall of Fame.

Later, I merged the Baechtold club with the fan clubs for Kenny Sears and Ray Felix and made one giant New York Knicks Fan Club, of which I was the first president. Thank you. In fact, the only reason I kept taking piano and accordion lessons at all was because my piano teacher, Mr. Karlin, had an excellent mimeograph machine. As long as I was taking lessons from him, he'd let me run off copies of our bulletin, "Knick Knacks." As you can see, I was not a normal child. I was possibly the only ball boy in NBA history whose hero was not on the bench but was instead the radio play-by-play guy over there with the gravy stain on his tie.

Anyway, that got me the ball boy job. I suppose I could have gotten some mileage out of all these jobs with the girls if I ever thought twice about girls then, which I didn't. I had a crush on the spotlight. All I wanted was to be discovered. I wanted the TV exposure. If there was a wet spot on the floor, I was the first one out there to wipe it up. A sure way to grab some TV time. If there was a team huddle during a time-out, I'd be the one hanging around looking for the right camera angle to get my face in the shot.

What I probably didn't realize was how few people actually gave a prune pit about the Knicks in the first place. In those days, the Knicks weren't enormously popular. Anytime the circus or the dog show came to Madison Square Garden, the Knicks got bumped to the 69th Regiment Armory, a converted military installation. The armory was to great basketball arenas what Velveeta is to the great cheeses of Europe. Often, there weren't any towels or soap for the players. You could tell the veterans in the league. They were the ones who brought their own soap on the New York trip. In fact, the visiting locker room, which I had to work plenty, resembled a high school shower room. The lockers were basically a folding chair and a nail on the wall. It was so cold in the armory that onetime Celtic Togo Palazzi wore gloves while on the bench. I *know* you've heard of Togo Palazzi.

The multimillion-dollar power forward hadn't been invented yet. One night, I was working the Syracuse Nationals locker room, which was just across from a refreshment stand. There was a security guard outside the door, but for some reason a fan walked right in, thinking it was the men's room. He stepped up to a urinal between the All-Star Dolph Schayes and head coach Paul Seymour. They looked at this guy in disbelief, but he innocently took care of himself and left without batting an eye. Today, you know that man as . . . German President Helmut Kohl. No, no, no.

Those were incredible days. Here I was 15 years old, the year was 1958, and I was taking a one-hour subway ride back and forth to Manhattan every night, getting home at 1 in the morning. I'd do my homework on the subway. Try that today. You'd end up as a smudge mark somewhere in the Bronx.

We'd play three-on-three until the players got there, then hang around with whoever might drop by: Wilt Chamberlain, Bob Pettit, Bill Russell, whoever. Some days they'd have doubleheaders at the Garden, maybe Boston against the Lakers and then the Knicks vs. the St. Louis Hawks. Sometimes between game days there would be a major concert, so they'd have a lot of the orchestra equipment backstage. Between games once, Cliff Hagan, a star of the St. Louis Hawks, sat down at the piano and knocked out some wonderful stuff. I'll never forget that: standing around a piano backstage at the Garden while an NBA standout in full uniform sat tickling the ivories. It was wonderful. Although, come to think of it, he never even *tried* "Malagueña."

I knew them all. Bob Cousy, Frank Ramsey, Jim Loscutoff, Easy Ed Macauley. They used to list Pettit as 6-10, but I saw him a few years ago and either I hit a growth spurt or he shrank, but Bob Pettit was no 6-10. He seemed 6-7, tops. Funny, I remember as a kid him being at least 7 feet.

I spilled water on all the greats. Wilt, Johnny Kerr, Larry Costello. I used to hear Russell throwing up before the game. Red Auerbach would throw me out of his locker room when I'd try to hang around and hear his pre-game talk. I knew Nat (Sweetwater) Clifton, one of the first black players in the NBA. They called him Sweetwater because he loved soft drinks. He was a very nice man in the locker room, but on the court he was like Willis Reed: Everybody feared him. He had one fight where he just demolished the guy and nobody tried him again. He had been a star with the Globetrotters before the Knicks. He died in the cab he drove for years in Chicago.

I had no idea then about racism. I had no idea that in those days if you were a black and weren't a starter, you had little chance to make the team. In fact, NBA teams had an unwritten rule that there were only so many blacks you could have on your roster. (Cal Ramsey, who would later become my color commentator for several years on the Knicks broadcasts, was waived in 1960 when he should have made the team. Obviously talented, he played in only seven games as a Knick and lasted only two years in the league.) All I knew is that the Globetrotters had an outstanding team. They used to play the NBA champs in a best-of-seven series and took the Lakers to seven games once. That's taking the Lakers to a seventh game without much coaching (Abe Saperstein was 90 percent road manager, 10 percent coach), with a ridiculously exhausting road schedule and spending most of their time working on their comedy bits. There is no question in my mind now that at one point in the late 1940s, the Globetrotters were one of the finest pro teams in basketball—NBA or not.

Sweetwater would give me a tip now and then. A good night's worth of tips was five dollars. That blew our friends' minds. Getting to sit on the bench of an NBA team *and* getting a tip? Get serious. As it turned out, two of the other ball boys that worked with me were more interested in "tips" than I was. Fred Portnoy ended up playing for Columbia and getting implicated in a college basketball point-shaving scandal. Also implicated was another ball boy who worked with me in those days, Artie Mandell. I suppose they made a lot of contacts at the Garden because in those days the Garden hosted many attractive college games. Portnoy admitted to taking $1,000 to keep his team's score down in a game with Rutgers in 1961. Mandell reportedly introduced Portnoy to the fixer, Joe Green. Apparently, they told him he could eventually make as much as $20,000. "I had that twenty-thousand figure in my head," Portnoy told the papers. "By the time I graduated, I could go into any business." The fixer, Joe Green, would pressure Mandell, and Mandell would pressure Portnoy. Portnoy finally agreed. Columbia was supposed to lose by 12. Portnoy made sure they lost by 13. In the end, Portnoy couldn't stand the guilt and told his father. He never spent the $1,000.

I made my own contacts through that job. The best one might have been Marty Glickman, the most well-respected sportscaster in New York when I was growing up. He was the Knicks' former play-by-play man and onetime voice of the New York Giants and New York Jets. Did you know Jack Kerouac mentions Marty in *On the Road?* You can look it up. I must have pestered that poor man to within an inch of his life, because he finally started letting me do stats for him during games. From then on, everything I did or said, I did or said like Marty Glickman. If he twitched, I twitched. If he had two lumps with his coffee, I had two lumps with my coffee. I wrote copy like he wrote copy. I was his alter ego.

Sometimes I wonder what my style would have been like if it weren't for Marty. He hated clichés and hype and I learned to hate clichés and hype. He was the eyes of the listener, so I tried to be the eyes of the listener. He followed the ball. He developed a geography of the court. You bring it up along the right sideline. You cross the half-court line, you come across the lane. He brought forth the language of the game. For instance, he was the first basketball announcer to start using the word "swish." People thought he invented it, but all he did was stand alongside Knicks star Carl Braun one day and every time Braun shot it up Braun would say, "Swish." He just brought it to the booth. And the country.

Marty Glickman was a superb athlete himself. He was on the United States track team at the 1936 Olympics in Berlin and was there each time Hitler would snub Jesse Owens because he was not blond and blue-eyed. "When we marched in for the Opening Ceremonies," Marty told me, "we all looked at him. There he was glaring down at us. And you could hear the whispering all through the ranks. 'He looks just like Charlie Chaplin!' " The irony, Marty said, was that Jesse was loved by the German people; loved so much that he had to take side entrances into and out of the stadium or be mobbed by worshippers. "Oh-vens!" they'd yell. "Oh-vens!" Owens was an embarrassment to Hitler in that he was quite obviously smashing Hitler's myth of Aryan supremacy. Every time he won a gold medal, Hitler would leave his perch.

Marty became a footnote in Olympic history in Berlin. He and another Jewish sprinter, Sam Stoller, were supposed to run in the 400-meter relay with Foy Draper and Frank Wykoff. Owens was not supposed to run. He hadn't touched a baton in weeks. Not that it mattered. The Americans were the hands-down favorites to win even without Owens. But, inexplicably, the American officials told Marty and Stoller, the only two Jewish runners on the track team, that they could not run. Their excuse was that they believed the Germans were "hiding out" their most powerful sprinters—sprinters nobody had ever heard of—and were going to spring them in the relay. Right. It was an obvious crock of bull. Marty and others always believed that Avery Brundage, USOC president at the time, was behind it. Brundage was known to be soft on Nazis. He was later one of the founders and organizers of the America First Committee, an organization some believed to be racist. Marty believed Brundage didn't want to further embarrass Hitler by first putting blacks on the medal stand and then Jews.

Owens even bristled. He said, "Coach, I'm tired. Let Marty and Sam run." But he was rebuffed. "You'll do as you're told," the coaches said. Marty and Stoller were out. Owens and Ralph Metcalfe were in. The controversy was huge. The Americans won anyway, as they would have with the Jewish runners. But every four years now, Marty is remembered as one of the most famous Olympians in history who never ran a race.

When they came home, the entire team received a ticker-tape parade in New York. Owens even rode in a convertible with Mayor Fiorello La Guardia. And yet, when the parade was over, Owens was still treated with disrespect in his own country. He wasn't allowed to stay above the second floor in some of the hotels other athletes stayed in and was made to use the freight elevator. Still, to the end, Jesse and Marty remained good friends.

So Marty was my hero, and since he went to Syracuse University, I went to Syracuse (so did Bob Costas, Dick Stockton, Len Berman, Andy Musser, Hank Greenwald, Neil Funk, Sean McDonough, among others). Naturally, the first place a sports microphone junkie like me got a job was at a classical music station, WONO-FM. Still, I was a freshman in college, opening up a radio station, throwing the switch and "starting the broadcasting day." You had to put bricks in my pockets to hold me down. Of course, I was much too hyper for any self-respecting Mozart dispensary. I'd come out of Vivaldi and go hard into American and National League action. I mean complete scores: winning and losing pitchers, batteries, stolen bases, home runs and RBIs. I'm sure your average longhair fan was really into knowing that Ernie Banks doubled off the wall in the fourth. I was quickly and rightfully fired.

Then came my rock era. I spun records as the coolest d.j. in town on radio station WOLF. They said my name wouldn't work too well on the air, so I changed it to Lance Scott. Even today, once in a while, a couple of guys I keep in touch with refer to me as Lance. To this day, I occasionally check into hotels as Lance Scott so Mike Fratello doesn't bother me.

I was suddenly a monster d.j., doing my Murray the K and Cousin Brucie impressions, using the dreaded echo chamber and running contests. Another disc jockey, Tricky Dick Snyder, and I went into business bringing major stars to Syracuse and presenting concerts. I booked Chubby Checker, Del Shannon, Bobby Vee, the Belmonts, and the Skyliners. To this day, if you name me a song, I can tell you the record company that made it, the flip-side title and the artist. I have more useless information in my head than a Braniff computer.

Eventually, the local Triple A baseball team, the Syracuse Chiefs, had an opening. I auditioned and got the job as the second man in the booth. My dad changed the family name to Albert then because he knew that would make life a lot easier for all of us. He kept Aufrichtig over the grocery store. My brother Steve, then in the seventh grade, was a little confused. He thought his name was now Albert Aufrichtig. He was not a quick study.

We'd do the home Chiefs games live, but we'd have to re-create the road games. All of a sudden, it was like I was back at WMPA, with my brother Al doing color and my brother Steve hitting a block of wood with a pencil for a base hit. I'm telling you, I was born to do this. We even had a crowd record given to me by Les Keiter, the popular New York announcer who did terrific re-creations of Dodgers and Giants games after they left New York for California.

We learned as we went. It didn't matter to us if I opened the game saying it was "another bright, sunny day" and then, ten minutes later, when the wire got stuck, said there was a "horrible downpour." Integrity was not a big priority in those days.

By my junior year, Marty Glickman offered me a job with him at WCBS radio in New York. He was broadcasting not only the Knicks but the football Giants for another station, *plus* his regular sports show, *plus* the Yankees pre-game and post-game shows. His producer-writer left for another station, so he offered the position to me. Do you remember those cartoon scenes when the character runs off in a such a hurry that all there is left is a few pieces of paper, stirred up from his whiplash departure, falling slowly, gracefully back to earth? Well, that's what my room looked like when I got the call. I think I left the phone dangling while I ran out of the room for the first plane back, my school papers floating gracefully back to earth. I finished college at New York University.

And then a wondrous, unbelievable, serendipitous thing happened. January 1963. Marty was in France at a harness race and became snowed in. The news director of WCBS called me in the early evening. "Can you do the Knicks game in Boston tomorrow afternoon?" Phone left dangling. Papers falling gracefully to earth. I have loved French harness racing ever since. My dad rushed me and brother Al (he'd do stats for me) to Grand Central to get the all-night milk train to Boston. My palms were sweaty and my breath short. Station WMPA had a collective heartbeat of 220. I was 20 years old. Al was 14. We could've run to Boston.

Unfortunately, when we arrived at the Garden, the guard wouldn't let us in. I don't suppose either of us looked like Red Barber. *Right. You're calling the Knicks game. And I'm Jacqueline Kennedy.* The guy would not budge. We pleaded with him. Zippo. I even opened up my briefcase and showed him all my commercials and note sheets. He said anybody could have that. Yes, I'll bet half the fans in Boston were running around with WCBS commercials in their briefcases. There were only forty-five minutes until game time when we finally convinced him to call over Knicks' general manager Eddie Donovan to vouch for us. That guard took ten years off my life.

Still, that was the scariest part of the whole trip. After that, it was just another call from our bedroom window, with the Boston Garden replacing Kensington Street and the Knicks and Celtics replacing the neighborhood stoopball game. I listened to that tape recently, and it cracks me up. When I hear it, I can't believe they allowed me on the air. Here was a college kid from NYU doing what sounded like a bad impression of Marty.

Suddenly, the world was at my feet. I started filling in on New York Rangers broadcasts too. Within three years, I had the full-time job as radio voice of the Rangers, and in 1967 the station offered me the Knicks radio job as well.

It had happened. I was now going to be the broadcaster for *both* the Rangers and the Knicks. It wasn't much, only every dream I'd ever had.

I went home to my apartment. I closed the door very calmly. And I screamed as loud and as hard and as long as I could.

One of the things that always bothered me was that people would come up to me and say, "Bill, don't you think Marv is great broadcasting those Knicks games?" I'd say to them, "How do I know? I never hear him—I'm on the court playing."

And they'd say, "Well, it goes something like this . . . 'DeBusschere down the lane, dishes outside to Bradley, over to Frazier . . . Yesssss!'"

If that's it, if that's all there was, then I'd say only one thing. He was vastly overrated.

—SENATOR BILL BRADLEY

3

All the Senator's Men

There are championship seasons and there are championship seasons, but the 1969–70 New York Knicks' championship season never seems to yellow.

People remember it like it was last week. Perfect strangers who lived their whole lives in far-flung parts of the country will come up to me and run down every name on the roster. Fans come up to me once a week and recall almost exactly the call of some indelible moment from that year. The names from that season never seem to fade: Reed, Frazier, DeBusschere, Bradley. The great moments from that season—Reed limping out to the jump-ball circle in Game 7—all still live. Even some of the fans became linked forever to that team—Woody Allen, Robert Redford, Elliott Gould, Dustin Hoffman. They'd be there nearly every night. William Goldman, screenwriter of *Butch Cassidy and the Sundance Kid,* refused to go the Academy Awards that year for fear of missing a good game.

I'd Love to But I Have a Game

In those days, maybe 30 games a year were on TV, and since nearly every game was a sellout, the only way someone could follow the team was on radio. And so I became linked forever with that team too. The radio audience grew and grew and my phrases and style seemed to catch on. For Game 7 of the finals, the radio audience was estimated at over one million, which was believed to be a record for a regional audience.

That was the most well-meshed team I've ever watched on the court and not the least bit close off it. It was basically twelve players, twelve cabs after the game. It was a disparate collection of players, politically, economically and socially.

You had the liberal intellectual, the million-dollar kid, Bill Bradley, who brought bags full of books on road trips. The future senator was constantly reading, on buses, on planes, in coffee shops, wherever. Often he would read in the locker room before the game. He was not a slave to fashion. His idea of travel dress was a pair of jeans and a white undershirt and a pair of socks with a hole in it. His locker was a mess. It was basically a pile of books, mail, papers, shoes, jocks, socks and paper clips. And yet he had his life wonderfully together. He was one of the most ethical persons I ever knew. He refused to do endorsements at all. "Why should somebody else use a product just because I tell them to?" He abhorred the cosmetic industry. To him, cosmetics included hair spray, cologne, makeup, whatever. He felt that Americans were overly concerned with "covering up" who they were. Remember the TV commercial where all the Knicks starters greet rookie Donnie May with low fives during player introductions? They all get grease on their hands and check his hair. It's greasy. They send him back to the bench until he learns to use Vitalis. Bradley refused to do it.

He was brilliant. The son of a well-to-do banker, Bradley was a Rhodes scholar, a Princeton man. He was a first-round draft choice of the Knicks, the College Player of the Year, yet he chose to study at Oxford and turn his back on the monster dollars the Knicks set out for him. Bradley didn't need basketball as much as basketball needed him. New York *Post* columnist Milton Gross wrote at the time that Bill Bradley might be the next President of the United States. Still might.

I honestly believe Bradley wanted to play pro ball from the beginning—he loved basketball—but was the sort of man who enjoyed depriving himself of pleasure because he knew it would make him stronger. He was into technique more than glory, team more than individuals, practice as much as games. He played more great basketball *without* the ball than anybody I ever saw.

He played on an Italian amateur league team just for the travel, but the day he knew he wanted to come back to basketball he was in a gym by himself. He was working out and began thinking about situations in a real game. He would do play-by-play as he pretended, with him taking the final shot or making the clutch free throw. The more he pretended, the more he wanted the reality. He told the Knicks he wanted to try it. Later, I asked to hear his play-by-play. He said he would let me, but it would break my heart.

Bradley had incredible eyes. Just by looking at it, he could tell whether a hoop was exactly 10 feet high. One time at Cobo Arena in Detroit, he walked in and said, "That basket is low." They checked it out and it was—one-quarter of an inch. He could also tell by sight if a ball was too inflated or deflated. He carried around with him a little pin used to inflate basketballs. One game, he insisted to the refs that the ball was pumped up too much just by a tiny bit. "Hey, we check these things out before the game," they said. But during a time-out that night, I saw him sneak the ball over to the bench and deflate it just for a second with his pin. Bradley had an overpowering sense of what was right.

His best friend on the team was Dave DeBusschere. In fact, Bradley and DeBusschere were probably the only two close friends on the club. Along with reserve Phil Jackson, they made up the liberal coalition on the roster. Bradley and DeBusschere, in fact, once went to an antiwar protest and march in Cincinnati on a road trip. Still, it was an odd friendship in that they seemed to have nothing in common. DeBusschere was a beer-drinking lunchpail kind of guy who did the dirty work and thanked you afterward. He was probably the most respected athlete on the team by the other athletes. He was tough and yet he was quiet. Incredibly, several years earlier DeBusschere was a player-coach for the Detroit Pistons at 24 years old.

DeBusschere was the best defensive forward in basketball. I remember the night Julius Erving played for the first time against the Knicks. In the ABA, Dr. J was a god. So when the Knicks and the New York Nets set up some exhibition games before the NBA-ABA merger, all eyes were on Dr. J, the unstoppable force, against DeBusschere, the glass wall. For DeBusschere, it was a huge game. He wanted to prove a point. Defense rarely gets its moment in the spotlight, yet here it was, his chance to prove what he could do. They played at the Garden. Erving rarely got a shot off in the first half. DeBusschere totally shut him down. It's the same way—the only way—to try and stop Michael Jordan nowadays. He can't score if he never gets the ball.

The most attractive personality on the team was Walt (Clyde) Frazier. He got the Clyde tag from backup center Nate Bowman, who thought Walt was smooth and slick as Warren Beatty's Clyde in the movie *Bonnie and Clyde*. And Frazier was consummate cool. He was a modern-day Beau Brummel. Clyde bought so many fine clothes that he had to build in extra clothes racks in the Manhattan hotel room he called home during the season earlier in his career. He was always the center of some magazine spread or another, lying on his huge round bed or riding in his chauffeur-driven Rolls-Royce, a beautiful babe or two on his arms. He had his own hairstyling salon. He was a reporter's favorite quote. He would say that he was so quick the flies had stopped flying near him for fear of being caught one-handed. He boasted that he could steal hubcaps off a moving car.

But Frazier always referred to that flamboyant person as Clyde and himself as Walt. Underneath, I think he was actually quite a shy person. His sister died of a drug overdose. He knew the price of indulgence. Sure, he would do his bit and go to the clubs, but I'm not sure that's who he really was inside. I say that because he is currently the radio analyst on Knicks games and he is nothing like that now. He is conservative and well spoken, a reader and a thinker. He wanted to improve as a broadcaster so badly that he read a thesaurus cover to cover to increase his vocabulary. He used to write five new words a day on his bathroom mirror so he couldn't help but work on them. You rarely see him in the hotel bar or at the clubs. Talk about change. He's so healthy he now brings his own food on airplanes.

And then there was Willis Reed, the Captain, who seemed not so much to be born great as to will himself great. Unlike Bradley, the son of a banker, Reed was raised on a poor Louisiana farm, chopping cotton. He was the most competitive player I ever knew. Even being drafted in the second round by the Knicks incensed him. "I can't believe they thought there were that many men who were better than me!" On the court, he never smiled and never backed off. His nose was broken five times and he always seemed to be gunning for six. In the first game of his third season, 1966, three Lakers jumped him and knocked him down. He came up swinging. He hit Rudy LaRusso twice in the mouth, broke John Block's nose and sent Darrel Imhoff down. He was so out of control, police had to intervene. Once that story got around the league, people were intimidated by him. Kareem Abdul-Jabbar was one who I think was literally afraid of having Reed rearrange his dental work. Whenever Kareem played against New York, he had some of his worst games. I think Reed peopled his dreams.

Finally, coming off the bench, there was Cazzie Russell, the Michigan All-American. Russell was flashy and streaky and loaded with talent. He worked harder on his body than anybody on that team. He was a health nut before anybody knew what a health nut was. He used to work out at the Y even after practices. Chris Mullin of the Golden State Warriors is famous for doing that now, but then it was unheard of. I remember Russell always carried his mystery bag with him on trips. I looked in it once. It was full of jars of wheat germ, honey, every kind of vitamin, diet supplements, body oils and lotions. The guys called him Max Factor. He could take it. He was the team comedian, the guy who kept everybody else loose. He could do a perfect Harry Caray. In fact, he could do a better me than me.

Anyway, when that group played together, which was often, they were a joy to watch. That team didn't rank in the Top 10 in any offensive category, but it did lead the league in one defensive one: fewest points allowed. That became coach Red Holzman's unbreakable commandment and the players' nightly goal: Hold the opponent to under 100. It was a perfect style for the players Holzman had and, coincidentally, it was the perfect style for me. They were so aggressive you could never back off the mike. My quick-delivery style was suited for the quick pace. With Clyde darting around trying to make steals, and DeBusschere causing all kinds of havoc, with passing so quick, the fans could not relax and neither could I. You look away for a moment and you might miss three buckets. Better yet, nearly every game became a sell-out. And even when the games were televised, they were usually tape-delayed, so you knew every kid and every Knicks fan with an antenna was listening to the live radio call.

That team started 23–1, a new record in the NBA, and it was no wonder. Aside from their basketball talent it was the smartest team I'd ever been around. With those four guys—Bradley, Reed, Frazier, and DeBusschere—plus Dick Barnett, it really was like having five coaches on the floor. One became a senator, two became coaches, one became a color analyst and Barnett, the fifth, was vastly underrated—he's the only one who earned a Ph.D. Four out of those starting five ended up in the Hall of Fame, everybody except Barnett. Oh, and Phil Jackson became a pretty decent coach too. Mike Riordan was a smart seventh man. He'd come in and give strategic fouls. There were also Dave Stallworth, the late backup Nate Bowman, Donnie May, Johnny Warren, and Bill Hosket.

I bring all their names up because they played probably the greatest seven-game series in NBA championship history. Set against a violent period of unrest, demonstrations, bombings, and protests over the Vietnam War, Jerry West, Wilt Chamberlain, Elgin Baylor and the Los Angeles Lakers came up against the Knicks to play some heated games. Clearly, these were the two best teams in the league in years.

The series was tied 2–2 when Reed started complaining about

his aching knees. Willis Reed wouldn't complain with a javelin protruding from his sternum, so you knew he was in pain. "The longer this goes on," he said, "the worse I'll be."

People talk about the seventh game of that series as unforgettable, but the fifth game, for me, was more so. It was May 4, 1970, the day of the Kent State shootings. My brother Steve was attending Kent State at the time. We were receiving sketchy reports over the wire and I was getting concerned. Steve worked on the college radio station there, so we knew there was a chance he was at the site when the shootings started. Four dead in Ohio. The wires weren't naming names yet. Finally, I had to leave for the game without knowing.

As it turns out, Steve wasn't at the site, but he was very close. Talk about surreal. He was sitting in a child psychology class adjacent to the Commons where the shooting occurred. It was around noon. The lights were out and the drapes were drawn in the classroom because they were watching a movie. In it, there were babies crying. The crying drowned out the gunshots. When the shades went up, they couldn't help notice ambulance after ambulance pulling up. Steve knew something was wrong. The Friday night before, an old ROTC building in the town of Kent, Ohio, was burned down as a Vietnam War protest.

He ran out of the classroom and saw the smoke from the gunfire just settling. People were running around madly. Steve ran to his dormitory to get his recorder, but there was an announcement on the public-address system. "Grab anything you can and please, get off this campus." They were closing down the school. Nobody was sure what would happen next.

Steve grabbed a tape recorder and some underwear, stuffed them in a satchel and started hitchhiking to Akron. He got a ride to the airport and caught the first flight to New York. He never had time to call.

Back in New York, the crucial game of the series tipped off. In the first quarter, Reed went down writhing in pain with a pulled muscle in his hip. Not only was he out of the game, he looked out for the year. Before you knew it, the Knicks trailed at halftime by 15. If they lost, they'd be down 3–2 for Game 6 in Los

Angeles. Good luck. To a man, every Knick thought the season was over. Frazier told me later his first reaction was "There goes the championship."

And yet, somehow, the Knicks came back. DeBusschere opened the second half with two long jumpers, creating the possibility in Laker heads that if the Knicks kept hitting from the George Washington Bridge like this, it didn't matter if they had Godzilla at center. For his part, Holzman sent a swarm of gnats at the giant Chamberlain: four different centers—DeBusschere ("I couldn't even see the top of him"), the rarely used Stallworth (who was maybe 6-7, tops), the seldom used Nate Bowman (the 6-11 backup) and forward Bill Hosket.

They hung on. Russell got hot and then Stallworth—of all people—started bombing jumpers over Chamberlain from outside. Suddenly, the Knicks were within one point.

Bradley took care of the rest. Stallworth was superb, too, outscoring Chamberlain 10–0 in his stints, the game of his life. The Knicks won 107–100 and I've never heard the Garden louder, before or since.

When I got off the air, dripping, I called my parents. They told me any minute now they were about to get an odd visitor in their living room: Steve.

L.A.'s win in Game 6 set up Game 7 at the Garden. Everybody in the city of New York wanted to know one thing: Would Willis play? Several hours before the game, in the Knicks locker room, I interviewed Willis for the pre-game show. He had been undergoing six hours of treatment every day since the injury, but when I arrived there, he looked like a man late for traction. He was dragging that leg around like it didn't belong to him. He was trying to jog lightly, but it looked hopeless. Still, I ventured forth the question: "Willis, will you be able to play tonight?"

And Willis Reed said, "I'll be out there, even if I'm on one leg."

It was certainly an appealing sound bite, but I didn't believe it for a second. The feeling around the front office was that this was the end of the line. Everybody off.

The Knicks began to warm up and still no Reed. I'd told my

50

radio-show audience at 5:30 that night that he *would* play. In the locker room, Reed was receiving a cortisone shot and Carbocaine for his hip. Still, it looked doubtful.

Then, suddenly, dramatically, Willis appeared on the court for the final minutes of warm-ups. The jolt of electricity that went through the crowd was like nothing I'd ever felt before. From my perch 200 feet above the court, I suddenly found myself doing play-by-play of the *warm-ups*. "Willis at the scorer's table. Willis has picked up a basketball." Every eye in the place was on him, including all the Lakers, who had turned around to look. He took a shot. "Yesssss," I said. "Willis has hit his first practice shot from fifteen feet away." And the crowd was going wild. "Here's the second one . . . Yesssss!"

The Garden was shaking with noise. And of course Willis started that game at center—on one leg. When his name was announced as a starter, you couldn't hear yourself gulp. Willis merely took two steps toward the huddle and sat back on the bench. Every step tonight was precious. He lined up at the center jump and didn't even move. Still, there were things he could do. He could lean his 240 pounds on Wilt. At the other end, he could take a pass from DeBusschere at the foul line, just as he'd done in warm-ups, and swish it. The score was 2–0 and you'd have thought Reed had just personally taken Saigon. He made his second. Pandemonium.

As the leg started to hurt more, Reed merely used himself as a screen. Still, the Knicks, using the huge emotional lift that Reed gave them, took a 17–8 lead. Reed was nothing but a placebo. Every Knicks fan knew Reed was going to come out soon. But to the Knicks players, it was like a miracle drug coursing through their veins. They played miraculously, and as they did, I suddenly felt like the old ball boy again, my heart rising and falling with every basket. By halftime, it was really over.

Knicks fans will forever remember Reed's heroics, but it was Walt Frazier who won that title. He played the greatest game of his life—36 points, 19 assists, 12 of 12 from the line, 12 of 17 from the field, inspired defense. He had accounted for 74 of the Knicks' 113 points. It was one of the most remarkable performances in seventh game history and it is still, to this day, pretty much forgotten.

In his book *Dream Team,* author Lewis Cole asked Frazier about it. "It was probably the greatest game of my career and it was a game that mattered—not just any game, but the last decisive game of the championship. But the next day, I don't read about *that* in the paper, but about Willis Reed because he sank two baskets. I was hurt." Can't say I would've blamed him.

And so it happened. I'm pretty cynical these days, pretty thick-skinned, but even now, when I hear that championship call— "DeBusschere holds the ball. Two seconds. DeBusschere holds the ball. One second. DeBusschere holds the ball. That's it! The Knicks are the world champions of the NBA"—I get goose bumps the size of grapes.

Great bar bet: The Knicks won that game with only four players on the court at the end. Fearful of being mobbed, Frazier had run into the safe haven of the locker room with four seconds left.

The Knicks won it, 113–99. Fittingly, they'd kept their commandment holy. The Lakers never broke 100.

I am so very proud of Marv. I can't tell you how much I burst with pride the other night when Marv walked off with an Emmy. He just went up to the table and walked off with it, sort of shoving it under his coat without any of the ushers seeing him. It was just a remarkable, indelible moment for me.

—AL ALBERT

4

You Any Relation to Your Brother?

It always intrigues people to find out that three brothers could all be doing play-by-play in the NBA—me for the Knicks, my brother Al for the Denver Nuggets and my youngest brother, Steve, for the Golden State Warriors. Invariably, they ask if our father was in the business too. And the answer is no, he wasn't, but our mother used to do the Memphis Tams for Charles O. Finley in the old ABA. They usually nod their head for a while when they hear that and then say, "Hey . . . wait a minute!"

Scientists have never been able to explain how we ended up as one ninth of the NBA TV play-by-play broadcasters, except that living in our house in Brooklyn was like going to a broadcasting school, room and board included. If two of us were playing Ping-Pong in the basement, the third would be doing the play-by-play. Anything at all that happened in our lives was potential programming. We had two hamsters—Ambrose and Zachary, perhaps the two most beleaguered hamsters on the planet—and we'd use them to stage the chilling Hamster Olympics, with one guy running the poor hamsters through obstacle courses and 40-yard dashes and the other two providing the play-by-play and commentary. Few people know this, but our house was a pilot program for ESPN.

Had I been our parents, I might have moved out. When the games finally ended for the day on our street and the sun went down, we'd start re-creating games out of the box scores. We'd set up the tape recorder. I'd handle play-by-play, Al worked the crowd record and the commercials and Steve did the sound effects. If I recall, a base hit was Steve hitting a No. 2 Ticonderoga pencil off a butcher block borrowed from my dad's grocery store. Naturally, we never let Steve do any announcing. Instead, we just hit him a lot.

Steve was constantly getting abused, especially by Al. Al was the most athletic and also the bully, so he got away with a lot. He used to pinch Steve under the table. Steve would start to cry, and my parents, who didn't know why Steve was crying, would slam him to shut him up. The sad thing is, we got together two months ago and the same thing happened.

My father, Max, loved sports, but my late mother, Alida, was absolutely and completely uninterested in it. She'd try to right the course of our lives, but to no avail. She'd take us all to music recitals, art exhibits, ballet performances and the theater, but we'd sneak in a transistor and an earplug and listen to the game anyway. My dad kept doing it later after we were all in the business. He'd sneak in the radio just to listen to our games. The ushers loved him, because he'd keep them advised of the score.

After we got older, my mother just learned to accept the fact that we were never going to become Leonard Bernstein. When she'd come to one of our games, she'd bring along her knitting. If she was home without Max, she'd turn on whatever game any of us were doing that night, check to make sure we looked healthy and then change the channel. If Max was home with her, they'd watch together, but some nights, with only one TV, that was impossible. I might be doing a Rangers game, Al an Islanders game and Steve a New Jersey Nets game. This annoyed her.

"Why do they have to put them all on at once?" she'd say. "We can't listen to them all at once. It's spite. That's what it is." My dad would explain to her that, as far as any of us knew, it wasn't spite.

For a while in New York, you couldn't go three channels in any direction without stumbling over an Albert. I did sports for WNBC at 5 and 11, and Al handled it at 6. Later, Steve filled in for me at 6 and 11 on WNBC. For a time, Steve and Al alternated doing the sports at WWOR-TV. Al did the Islanders. Steve did the Islanders. Al did the Devils. Steve did the Devils. Al did the Nets. Steve did the Nets. Al had stomach trouble. Steve had stomach trouble. Which is one reason I never wanted to do the Nets.

One night, there was a game we *all* worked. Me for the Knicks, Steve for the Nets and Al for USA Network. I can't believe it ever happened before or since, three brothers all broadcasting the same game for three different companies. If you listened hard enough, you could hear all our voices going full throttle at once. Al said he half expected Mom to yell upstairs for us to shut the door.

People think it's a remarkable coincidence that we all got into sportscasting, but, actually, it was anything but. All of us *lived* for it. Everything we did was a step toward it. Take Steve. Steve deliberately picked Kent State because it had no hockey team. He knew he could go there, start one and be the announcer. And that's exactly what he did. He helped build the rink and then became the traveling secretary, president, public relations director and the voice of the Kent State Clippers. Steve is a *very* pushy person.

You have to love the business to stick it out through some of the places Steve worked. The first professional hockey broadcast he ever did was for the Cleveland Crusaders of the old World Hockey Association (Wayne Gretzky's first pro league) in 1972 at the old Cleveland Arena. He said it was like a scene out of the movie *Slap Shot*. The rink had chicken wire around it instead of Plexiglas and the fans used to sneak things through the holes in the chicken wire—like their fists. They'd try to grab the necks of the opponents as they went by. I am almost positive they didn't want autographs. Steve had to call the game from the end zone, and since hockey jerseys don't have numbers on the front, he had to memorize the faces of the players. When he didn't recognize a face, he faked it. Hey, it was radio.

It was during those years that Steve had his most embarrassing moment. In fact, Al and I voted it the most embarrassing moment in the history of the family. He had just gotten off one of these mind-bending road trips that only WHA teams would take—through the United States and Canada, 17 days, 14 cities, 439 warnings to bring your seat back to its full upright position. The night after they got back, they had a game at home and Steve's brain was scrambled like an omelette. It was the end of the first period and Steve needed to send it to a commercial, so he said, "So that's the end of the first period and the score is Cleveland 2 and . . . and . . . and . . ."

He'd completely forgotten who Cleveland was playing. He looked over at his engineer, who was in no position to help, as he had tears coming out of his eyes and was short of breath with hysterical laughter. He looked over at his statistician, who couldn't help him either. He was doubled over. He looked at the scoreboard. No help there either. All it read was "Home" and "Visitors." He looked at the players' jerseys but found no help there either. After what seemed like hours to him, he finally just gave up and said, "Folks, I cannot remember *who* Cleveland is playing." As soon as he said it, it came to him and he blurted it out: "The Chicago Cougars! Cleveland 2, the Chicago Cougars 1."

But it was too late. The thing had been done. That tape was played on the air about forty times that week in Ohio and managed to make its way around the country twice. Personally, I made a nifty distribution profit from it.

After that, Steve took over as the voice of the New York Nets of the ABA. That was the 1975–76 season, the year the Nets, behind Dr. J, beat Al's Nuggets, behind David Thompson, to win the last ABA title. That was a terrific series. That was the ABA's heyday, just before the merger. In fact, my brothers are part of a great basketball trivia question: What two brothers broadcast the final game in ABA history? It was Game 6 at Nassau Coliseum in Long Island. The Nuggets, trailing two games to three, led the Nets by 20 points late in the third quarter. It looked like the series was going back to Denver. That's when Nets coach Kevin Loughery sent out the storm troopers. Using his two bulky enforcers, John Williamson and Rich Jones, the Nets mounted an unbelievable comeback and won the title that night.

As the final seconds ticked down, so many fans swarmed the floor that Al had to stand on top of the press table to broadcast the close of the telecast. Unfortunately, Al had made too many trips to the press buffet that night and the table collapsed underneath them while they were on the air. They couldn't have wrapped up the Nuggets' collapse any better. Later, when the dust settled, everything of Al's was gone—notes, books, TV monitors, everything. Apparently, it's an old Long Island tradition. Anytime the home team wins a championship, the fans make off with the visiting team's TV monitors.

To this day, whenever they get together, Steve brags about the two times in his life when he beat Al at something. One was the Nets beating the Nuggets and two was the time at Camp Cayuga in Pennsylvania when his Red team beat Al's White team in capture-the-flag. And that was in 1991.

But those were the only glory days in Steve's 13 years with the Nets. The rest was a lot of 30-point blowouts starring Bubbles Hawkins. Not that losing teams couldn't be fun. On one trip to San Antonio, the players got on the bus to go over to HemisFair Arena and noticed that Rich Jones wasn't on it. He wasn't at the game either, even though everybody had seen him at the hotel that day. The truth was, Jones was *still* back at the hotel, locked in his room. Nets coach Kevin Loughery had locked him in because he'd gotten word that if Jones showed up at the arena, he was going to be arrested on an undisclosed Texas criminal charge. Forget jurisprudence, Loughery needed him the rest of the trip. So Rich watched the game on TV. Not bad work if you can get it.

Steve went through an Encyclopædia Britannica's worth of players on the Nets in those years. Still, each time a new one came, he'd go up and introduce himself. One day, the new Net was Leon Wood, the point guard from Cal State–Fullerton. Steve walked up, extended his hand and said, "Hi, I'm Steve Albert."

"Nice to meet you," said Wood. "Are you any relation to your brother, Marv?"

"Luckily, no," said Steve.

As if calling the Nets games wasn't punishment enough, Steve also did the morning sportscasts for WABC radio. He'd go on at 5:30, which meant leaving his apartment in Fort Lee, New Jersey, at 3:45. One particularly freezing morning, Steve got up and prepared to shower. This time, though, he closed the bathroom door behind him to let the steam from the shower warm up the bathroom. Not a good idea. The latch on that bathroom door had been acting funny and, on this particular day, it broke. Steve found that out after he'd shaved. He toweled off and was ready to walk back into his bedroom and start dressing when the bathroom door wouldn't open.

He jiggled the knob a dozen times. Nothing. The doorknob itself had come loose and was out of its socket. It was now 4:15 and he had to get across the bridge to do the morning sports. He was trapped. He tried to take the hinges off, but they were painted in solidly. Now it was 4:30. If he didn't get out of there soon, he was going to blow the sportscast. He panicked. He became inhuman. He took an aerosol hair-spray can and started hacking at the wooden door with it like a wild man. The door began to splinter, wood flying everywhere, until, finally, he had knocked a hole big enough to slip his hand through. He reached through to turn the doorknob on the outside. It still didn't work.

That's when he went bonkers, smashing the hole with the can, kicking and punching at the hole, screaming at the door. The neighbors, thinking somebody was getting murdered in his apartment, rolled over and went back to sleep. Hey, this was *New Jersey*. Finally, he got the hole big enough to get a leg through. Remember, he's naked. He gets one leg through and gets stuck.

I'd Love to But I Have a Game

By now, the splinters have made him a soprano. Wouldn't you have loved to see the scene? Here's one of Steve's legs and his, ahem, backside sticking through a hole and that's it. The average passerby might have thought it was some newfangled kind of bicycle rack.

Finally, he slipped back into the bathroom and, in a fit of rage, began kicking the smithereens out of the door until it was finally such a shambles he could simply walk right through it like Arnold Schwarzenegger. He threw on a suit and rushed to the studio. He barely made it on time. At the end of his broadcast, though, he told his story on the air. It was like a catharsis for the citizens of the tri-state area. People called in by the dozens with their own harrowing locked-in-the-bathroom stories. At the end of the day, though, everybody came to one conclusion. Steve's was still the stupidest.

Al probably would have busted through that door fifteen minutes faster. He was always the best jock in the family. He originally thought he'd be a professional hockey player himself and, in fact, for a time, was. He played goalie at Ohio University. But because he didn't start until his senior year, he asked his coach if he could announce the games on radio. The coach said O.K., as long as he was in uniform in case the first three goalies went down. That, too, must have been a very fine sight. My brother Al, sitting in press box, announcing the games fully dressed in his uniform and pads. But it was hard to keep from mixing the two jobs up. Somebody once dropped a doughnut near him and Al smothered it until he heard a whistle.

His pro hockey career began, believe it or not, in a New York Rangers camp. Al had high hopes until his first Rangers scrimmage, in which a guy named Wayne Rivers came in on a breakaway. Al stacked the pads perfectly, except Rivers put the puck on the crossbar and bounced it in for a goal. Welcome to the NHL, fella.

Al was shipped out to the Toledo Blades, an International Hockey League team, where he jumped off to a bit of a slow start. When his "goals against" average reached 90.46, he decided to change careers. The announcer's spot for the Blades was open and both he and his coach were *very* eager for him to take the job. I still thought it was bad form to continue to announce games in complete goalie uniform, though.

Al eventually called the New York Islanders games and then moved to Denver to do the Nuggets. As with Steve and the Nets, there haven't been a ton of Nuggets highlights to look back on, but the ones that exist have Al's voice attached to them. He was there the night David Thompson had 73 points the last game of the season in an attempt to win the scoring title. Incredibly, Thompson had 50 at halftime. Unfortunately George (Iceman) Gervin of San Antonio scored 63 later that night to hang on and win it. It is known in basketball as the day Defense Took a Holiday.

Of course, Al made his own mark on the game. Who can forget the time the Nuggets came to the Houston Summit to play the Rockets? Al decided he no longer needed to open glass doors and instead chose to jog smack into one. Al has done a lot of boxing in his life, but it wasn't until that day he knew the joys of a mandatory eight count. He actually had to lie down in the Nuggets training room and be cared for by the Nuggets doctors. And yet he worked the game that night, entirely spaced out and half unconscious. In Denver, they still remember it as one of his finest broadcasts. Turns out he had a concussion. Now, whenever he's at a big event and he sees a very nicely Windexed glass door, just out of sentiment, he will go barreling into it.

Maybe something jiggled in his brain that night, because ever since then Al has had a very sick sense of humor. One time, he did this bit on the evening sports in which he went to cover a man who could keep a soccer ball in the air with his head, shoulders, knees, feet for hours at a time. The man was very close to breaking the world record—he'd been going for almost twenty-four hours straight—when Al began the interview. "He's very close now," Al says, walking into the shot, looking at the camera. "He's at 25,146, now 25,147. Let's see if we can get a word in with Tommy." And as he turns to interview Tommy, Al's elbow hits the ball and it falls to the floor. Tommy just looks at him. Al got hate mail for weeks after that. Of course, my hand got *very* cramped.

All in all, I am extremely proud of my brothers for all that they've achieved. And I think it just goes to show you what good parole officers can do to turn people's lives around.

I would like to refute two myths. The first is the one about Marv and me growing up together in Brooklyn. This got started because our roots are in the same neighborhood. In reality, my first remembrance is a sponging-down by my mother in our bathroom with Marv's distinct tones washing out of the radio and over my precious pink body. I distinctly remember Marv saying, "My in-studio guest tonight will be Yankees rookie Tony Lazzeri."

The second fallacy deals with my call at the end of the U.S.-Soviet hockey game in the 1980 Lake Placid Winter Olympics. At the end of one of the most stunning upsets in the history of sport, I exclaimed, "Do you believe in miracles? Yes!"

Marv has recently told people that it's *his* voice answering my rhetorical question. This is what happens to guys who spend too much time at 37,000 feet. Minimal research reveals that at the time Marv was registered at the Motel 6 in Winnipeg for a Rangers-Jets game. The hotel's records show a Mr. Albert in Room 206 ordering two Ovaltines for breakfast and proffering a two and a half percent tip.

Nevertheless, all of us in this wacky trade owe Marv a great debt. As usual, he's trying to collect.

—AL MICHAELS

5

Birds, Bombs and Bernard

Twenty-five years after my first Knicks broadcast, I was honored and gratified to have my own night at Madison Square Garden. I must say I was thrilled at the excitement over the event. You could not get a ticket to that game for months in advance. The Garden was packed and nearly every newspaper and radio and TV outlet doubled their staffs for the game. There were some *feverishly jealous* types in the media who attributed all that to the fact that the Knicks were playing Michael Jordan and the Chicago Bulls that night. I call it sour grapes.

The most touching moment of the evening for me was when David Letterman, with the help of his very caring staff, presented the following:

TOP TEN REASONS WE'RE HONORING
MARV ALBERT TONIGHT

10. Even when he's excited, he doesn't spit much on the mike.

9. He doesn't know it, but he's only got two or three weeks to live.

8. His play-by-play of Wilt Chamberlain's 20,000th date.

7. Came off the bench to hit buzzer beater in Knicks' 1973 championship game.

6. His famous generosity, including his promise to give everyone in the Garden tonight fifty dollars in cash!

5. His entourage of hot-looking Marvettes.

4. His popular chicken cordon bleu sandwich.

3. On honeymoon, never violated the 24-second clock.

2. Has better hair than Pat Riley.

1. Is this a man worth honoring? Yesssss!

Then, my good friend and color analyst on Madison Square Garden Network, John Andariese, had a very thoughtful idea. He said that instead of raising a banner or something to the roof, they should raise *me*. In addition, NBA commissioner David Stern admitted to never having heard of me. Bob Costas sent a tape of every interview I'd ever done in which the athlete walked off in a huff. It was just an unforgettable evening.

In reality, my Knicks memories go further back than 25 years. For instance, I can remember Cleveland Buckner from Yazoo City, Mississippi. The roster said Buckner was about 6-9, but in reality he stood about 6-5, because wherever he went, he never stood up straight. He was always stooped over. Turns out he grew up in a house where the ceilings were very low. He needed either a good chiropractor or a 6-foot-and-under league.

I remember the night Gene Conley got a little hungry sitting on the bench during a game in Detroit in 1963. Conley was an average player who also once pitched in the major leagues and was considered a bit of a flake. Next thing anybody knew, they saw Gene standing in line for a hot dog at one of the concession booths. In full uniform . . . *during* the game!

65

I'd Love to But I Have a Game

Counting my ball-boy years, I have been around fourteen Knicks coaches, from Vince Boryla to Pat Riley, from 5-10 Red Holzman to 6-10 Willis Reed. From the high-decibel Hubie Brown to the low-decibel John MacLeod. At least you could hear what MacLeod was saying. Dick McGuire mumbled. The more excited he got, the more he mumbled. One time, McGuire called Walt Bellamy over to the sideline and gave him what looked like a passel of very involved directions and urgings. But when reporters asked him later what McGuire had said, Bellamy had to tell the truth. "I don't know. I couldn't understand a single word."

Nobody ever had that trouble with Hubie Brown. Not only could the players hear him, the people in the top-row seats could hear him too. Off the court, Hubie was a very personable guy— he went on to make an excellent color analyst—but the players didn't always appreciate his coaching style, his constant rantings and ravings at them, the way he called every play, the way he screamed at them after a mistake. Because of that, Knicks center Patrick Ewing and Brown got along like in-laws. One thing about Ewing, he hates getting yelled at. He never liked it when Bobby Knight yelled at him during the 1984 Los Angeles Olympics either. And so I felt he didn't always play hard for Hubie.

It's too bad, because Hubie was a genius with X's and O's and he was brilliant when it came to making average players overachieve. I always thought he would have been an outstanding college coach, because players are in school for their two, three or four years, then move on. The shorter exposure to volatile surroundings, the less extensive college schedule and the more impressionable younger players would have been an effective setting.

Still, I don't blame Hubie. He got killed by injuries. You'd walk into his locker room and you'd have thought you were in the waiting room at an HMO. Basically, what he had when you counted the people in uniform was a CBA team. This is a Knicks coach who *opened* seasons starting the likes of Ed Sherod and Ken (the Animal) Bannister. Sounds like a wrestling tag team.

When Bernard King went down with his knee injury in 1985, the Knicks got even worse. In Hubie Brown's last full year,

1985–86, they were 23–59. Before that, though, Bernard King provided the Knicks with some special moments. I called King's back-to-back 50-point games—January 31 (San Antonio) and February 1 (Dallas), 1984, on a Texas road swing. I always knew King could go ballistic any given night and score 70—that season, he'd hit 52 against the Pacers in November and 60 against the Nets on Christmas Day—but I never thought he'd do it back to back. And *the way* he did it was amazing, too—13 seconds left in Dallas and he makes a 15-footer for 50. His 32.9 scoring average that year hasn't been touched by anybody but Michael Jordan since.

Think about this: Had King not blown out his knee the next year, the Knicks could have had a starting front court of King, Ewing and Larry Bird. It's true. The late Sonny Werblin, the charismatic impresario and president of Madison Square Garden, had his chance at Bird. Werblin was a guy who didn't miss often. He's the man that signed Joe Namath to the New York Jets for a then unheard-of $400,000. But he blew this one. Bird was available for the 1978 draft after his junior year because he was a year behind his graduating class. I asked Werblin if he'd consider drafting him. "Nah," Werblin said. "Our people don't think he's going to be any good."

Selecting two spots after the Knicks, the Boston Celtics that year took Bird as a junior and wound up winning three titles with him. The Knicks took Micheal Ray Richardson, and won zero titles with him. I believe Sonny's "people" were the same ones who thought blue jeans were just a fad.

I went nine straight years—1979 through 1987—in which the Knicks never finished higher than third in the Atlantic Division. People would come up to me and say, "You poor thing." But, actually, I felt just the opposite. It's a genuine test for a broadcaster to try to keep it interesting. Bad teams can make for good punch lines.

Besides, half the fun over these 27 years in New York has been observing the scene at the Garden—all the characters. For years and years, the Knicks had the distinct booming voice of John Condon as their public-address announcer. Condon was also the

Garden boxing publicist and that meant he worked on some monumental fights. For instance, the first Muhammad Ali–Joe Frazier fight was at the Garden. Naturally, it was a sellout. Naturally, that didn't stop the fans from doing whatever they could to con their way inside. One guy came up with a good one. Carrying two pairs of boxing gloves, he convinced the security guards that these were the gloves for the fight and that it was imperative he get inside to deliver them to the fighters. The guy got as far as the elevator, where he ran into Condon.

"Where do you think you're going?" Condon asked.

"I'm assigned to bring the fighters their gloves," the man said with perfect aplomb. "I'm afraid I'm going to have to ask you to stand aside. Time is of the essence."

"It certainly is," said Condon. "They're already in the second round."

Condon was the p.a. announcer the last time the Knicks played in an NBA finals, 1973, the year they won the title. But, for some reason, that title isn't nearly as memorable to New Yorkers as the world championship they won in 1969–70. Even to me it's not and I've never quite understood why. Maybe it was just that the first one was so unforgettable. Maybe it was because the chemistry was changed. Or maybe it was because the finals were such a walkover—four games to one over the Lakers.

The Knicks bottomed out early in the playoffs the year after their first title, then lost in the finals to the Lakers in 1971–72. By the 1972–73 season, guard Dick Barnett was getting long in the tooth and Willis Reed began to look like a M*A*S*H patient.

That's when the Knicks pulled off two stirring trades. First, they traded Cazzie Russell to the San Francisco Warriors for Jerry Lucas. The idea was that Lucas would assume Reed's mantle when Reed's bones finally gave out and could hit the boards as a power forward until then. He did that and more. Lucas added passing, outside shooting, some presence at center, some of the best outlet passes I've ever seen and "the Bomb," his dead-on long-range missile.

He also added a bit of oddity to the team. He was obsessed with his stats. He could compute in his mind what his new seasonal field-goal percentage would be on the way back down the court. He was not selfish. He just knew a lot of tricks to make his stats look better. At the end of quarters, he'd race to get a rebound nobody else cared about before time expired. He told me once if you could get two or three of those a night, you'd raise what would have been an ordinary five-rebound night to an eight-rebound night and it would pay off at negotiation time.

Lucas was always fascinated by odd facts and possibilities. He was widely known for magic tricks. He had a photographic memory. He claimed he could open the Manhattan telephone book to any name up to "E" and, without looking, recite the person's phone number. He kept win-loss records of the guys who played poker on Knicks flights. He wound up starting his own fast-food franchise, called Jerry Lucas's Beef 'n' Shakes. I'll bet he could tell just by looking how many straws were left in the straw dispenser.

The other trade was a steal: Mike Riordan and Dave Stallworth (two non-starters) plus cash for Baltimore's star guard, Earl (the Pearl) Monroe. When the trade went down, the Knicks players weren't so sure what they were getting. They were apprehensive about what kind of person Monroe was. Monroe had always been a mystery man, the sort of guy who keeps to himself, who just suddenly appears places and disappears just as quickly. He had that Garbo kind of mystery to him. Woody Allen, an avid Knicks fan, was mesmerized by him. He once wrote an article for *Sport* magazine about Monroe. He admitted how much he'd always wanted to interview Monroe. So, after ruminating and hesitating and intellectualizing about Monroe for half the article, he finally got his nerve up and went to Monroe's town house. When he got there, he was made to wait and wait and wait. Finally, after a very long time, Allen decided that the waiting made Monroe even more alluring in his eyes and left.

The end of that era came the day they traded Walt Frazier to Cleveland in 1977. Frazier was in a mediocre stretch of his career then. People just couldn't believe he couldn't play the way he had in the glory days. Some people accused him of jaking it. They said he nursed injuries. To Frazier, being traded to Cleveland was like being banished. He didn't get along with Cleveland coach Bill Fitch. He rebelled against Fitch's three-and-a-half-hour practices. "He was way too hard on guys," Frazier says. "He wouldn't talk to you if you lost the game or you were injured. Some days we'd practice *after* a game. On the bus after a loss, you were expected to look down, glumly. We were supposed to be like children."

Clyde was a man wearing the wrong uniform. I still remember the night he came back to the Garden for the first time in a Cavs jersey. Clyde was nervous about how the crowd would react to him. After all, remember, New York fans are about as sentimental as traffic cops. These are the same fans who booed their legendary hero Willis Reed when he coached the Knicks to, apparently, not enough wins.

When the night came and Frazier's name was announced, the sellout crowd gave him a standing ovation. Frazier bowed his head. But then a funny thing happened. The ovation wouldn't die. It kept getting louder and more raucous. Suddenly, the wave of emotion seemed to hit Frazier flush in the face. He raised his head, then his hands, then raised them high and exultant. Then he went out and had a sensational game, hitting a jumper to win it in overtime, raising those same hands, soaking up the feeling.

Somewhere in the Garden that night might have been a young future Knick named Mark Jackson, who also went through a love-hate relationship with New York fans. Jackson grew up idolizing Walt Frazier and there were times during his Knicks career when you felt that he wanted to be adored by the Garden crowds as much as they had adored Frazier. At first, you felt as though it could almost happen. He was Rookie of the Year in 1988. But by his third year, it began to go to his head. He was cocky. He was outrageously flamboyant—helicopter spins and showboating passes and celebratory gyrations. He became a headache to his team. Knicks coach Rick Pitino tried to curb him some, but he couldn't. Stu Jackson and John MacLeod tried too, and when they couldn't, they just benched him. By his fourth season, Jackson was completely out of the rotation.

But then the Knicks hired Pat Riley, and Pat Riley may have

saved Jackson's career. Unlike Pitino, Pat Riley absolutely, positively, puts up with zero bull. He is the complete professional. To Jackson's credit, he showed up for camp that next year in the best shape he could possibly be in. He completely re-geared himself to playing solid basketball. It was a complete turnaround. Later, though, when Jackson was traded to the L.A. Clippers, the Knicks played them for the first time and Jackson got into a trash-talking festival with the Knicks' John Starks, Anthony Mason and Greg Anthony. Starks even threw water at Jackson. Riley was so upset that he benched those three key players the next game, a move that is unheard of in the NBA. But he did it and got away with it and his players got the message.

Suddenly, for the first time since the early 1970s, the Knicks are again one of the elite teams in the NBA. Even the stars who pack Celebrity Row, the courtside seats across from the Knicks bench, are hounding the front office for tickets. Spike Lee, John McEnroe, Arnold Schwarzenegger, Dustin Hoffman, Michael Douglas, Michael Keaton—every night, it's loaded. And they're knowledgeable. William Goldman is nearly demented about the Knicks. Not only does he come to every game but afterwards he goes home and watches his tape of the game just to listen to what John and I said. No wonder there's not a lot of good movies out anymore.

Woody Allen is seriously into it too. During his legal entanglements with Mia Farrow, the *one* shot of Woody and Mia's 21-year-old daughter, Soon Yi, was taken at a Knicks game. I remember John Andariese and I used to glance over at them during time-outs and say to each other, "What a nice father-daughter relationship."

Sadly, very few of the celebrities that come to watch the Knicks seem overly enthused about meeting John. One night, Peter Falk, the actor who played Columbo all those years on television, got up from his seat during a time-out, looked right at John and started heading over. John got rather excited and started straightening his tie. Falk walked right up to him and said, "Excuse me, John?"

I'd Love to But I Have a Game

John, feigning surprise, turned and said, "Yes?"

"Uh, I just wanted to ask you something," Falk said.

"Yes?" said John eagerly.

"Well," he said, "I've got Ewing at two for seven from the field. Is that what you have him at?"

This is not widely known, but I used to do play-by-play myself. It was in South Dakota, doing mostly high school and college football and basketball. I wasn't great but I wasn't bad either. Except one time I realized I had the halftime score wrong, which meant I'd had the score wrong the entire game.

The only reason I bring this up is this: I want to do a job share with Marv. I'll do the Knicks-Bulls games, the NBA playoffs, the Olympics and the better NBC Games of the Week. He can have all the news nights when the biggest story is a bus hijacking in Peoria and a worldwide summit on whole life insurance.

—TOM BROKAW

6

Life Is a Non-title Bout in Maracaibo

All I can say about the Fight Doctor—Dr. Ferdie Pacheco—is that he is *not* the sort of physician you'd want at the bedside of a loved one.

Ferdie Pacheco is an astute analyst, but the man's quiet moments are rare. I once flew twenty-four hours straight with him to South Africa, taking three different planes, and not once, not ever, did Ferdie stop talking. At some point in his life, the man swallowed a Toastmasters convention. He is a very talented and diversified man—a cartoonist, an artist, a novelist, a playwright, an inventor, a sociopolitical expert, and he was, at one time, Muhammad Ali's personal physician—but sometimes I just have to say, "Hold on just a second, Ferdie. I've got to change ears."

Ferdie talks so much that he sometimes wears out one language and has to move to another. We were covering a fight in Italy once and, as usual, Ferdie was scheduled to do the post-fight interviews. On this particular fight, Ferdie had an Italian translator, but for some reason the translator didn't make it into the ring with him after the fight. It's always mass chaos in a boxing ring after a fight and everybody was screaming and yelling and carrying on. Still, Ferdie gave me the sign that he's ready and I said, "O.K., now let's go to Ferdie in the ring." And Ferdie, who speaks fluent Spanish, starts interviewing the guy in *Spanish*. Live, on the air, on network television. The man just lost it. The Italian fighter just looked at him like, "What in the world are you saying?" And you know what? It *still* ranks among Ferdie's best work.

David Letterman used to take great delight in asking me, "So, Marv, what non-title bout in Nigeria are you doing *this* week?" Which was an insult, of course. I've never done a non-title bout in Nigeria. I've done non-title bouts all over the world—including Maracaibo, Venezuela—but never Nigeria. In fact, that 1984 fight in Maracaibo was a benchmark of my career. On the undercard that day was a guy named Wilbert (Vampire) Johnson, who was carried by handlers out to the ring in a coffin. He was fighting John (the Beast) Mugabi, which prompted Ferdie to say, "In a couple of minutes, Wilbert might be *leaving* in a coffin." He was right. In the second round, the Vampire was knocked out.

The most nerve-wracking bout we ever telecast was in 1979 in Pretoria, South Africa. It was one of the first international sporting events allowed there in years because of the international sporting ban on that country. John Tate vs. South African Gerrie Coetzee. The racial tension that day was thick. There were 80,000 people there and maybe 500 of them were black. You were not sure at all what was going to happen: black man vs. white man in the very heart of apartheid. We were told they expected a bomb. There were police everywhere, armed with machine guns and flanked by snarling guard dogs. And yet it was mildly comic in that we were in an outdoor mud-floor arena. The ground was pure mud and I was wearing a tuxedo, no socks and sneakers. Ferdie was muttering about some plan to jump under the ring in case there was a riot. Good idea. In case there's a riot, there will be 9,000 people trying to climb into the ring. When it collapses on us, it'll take fourteen days for them to find us and bury us. To top it off, we also had Roberto Durán next to us, laughing hysterically. This was Roberto Durán's kind of situation: soldiers and guns and dogs and mud and fear. Lovely.

Luckily, nothing historic happened, except that Durán babbled to Ferdie in Spanish the whole time we were on the air and the closest we came to losing our lives was when somebody threw a sandwich that went zipping by our table. If I am going to die conducting overseas journalism, I do not want the cause of death to be a hard salami roll to the temple.

I still think Durán has been one of the most exciting athletes in sports. Even with the *no más* thing he pulled in the Sugar Ray Leonard fight, his image never really suffers. No matter what he's done, he seems to cut through any harsh feeling people might have about him. Nobody knows the real reason Durán quit against Leonard, and since he pretends he only speaks Spanish, he never had to answer the tough questions about it in this country. What's funny is I had a long conversation with him entirely in English in 1982. But a year later, when I was doing sports in New York, he walks into the studio with a Spanish interpreter. All of a sudden, it's *"No habla inglés."* Katarina Witt, the East German ice skater, was like that. For press conferences in the early 1980s, before the Sarajevo Olympics, she'd have what looked like a KGB agent there, her stern coach and an interpreter. And every question you'd ask, you'd get a two-word, useless answer. But then you'd see her giggling and speaking English with some English-speaking competitor. When the Berlin Wall fell, she spoke like she'd been studying at Stanford for six years.

To me, boxing has the best stories. Ever since my dad used to take me to the outdoor ring at Coney Island for the fights, I've loved it. I used to hide a radio under my sheets at night and listen to the fights. Even today, the one event I find the most thrilling is a heavyweight championship bout. The World Series and the NBA finals are great, but they're best of seven. This is *one* fight. I love the grand entrances, the multitudes of people in the ring, and then suddenly there are only three, trapped inside the ropes. As in no other sport, you can see the nervousness in their faces. Nothing hides them. They are in there in front of the world in their shorts, stripped of everything but their skills and their courage. It's unexplainably exciting.

Besides, for a journalist, boxers provide the best theater, hands down. They will say and do anything and usually have some unbelievable story to tell you, a good deal of which is sometimes true. They are usually wonderfully natural and colorful. One time Joe Louis was fighting an unknown named Arturo Godoy, a South American. Godoy came out of his corner for Round 1 all crouched over and scrambling around curiously like a stone crab. Louis looked at him for a moment and grinned. "Man fightin' me sideways," he explained afterwards.

You have to be a little skewed to fight. There was once a fighter named Bruce (the Mouse) Strauss. His claim to fame was being knocked out on every continent except Antarctica, and he was hopeful on that account. He was a paid stiff. A tomato can. Somebody who would get you an automatic win, one more that you needed to get your young fighter's record on its way to 20–0 or 25–1, so that the networks might take you. Strauss prided himself on his glass chin and weak knees. He was the best bum working. One night, Strauss fought in the second bout of a nine-bout card and was, naturally, knocked out. When he woke up in the dressing room, he heard the promoter talking to a manager in a panic. The heavyweight scheduled for the main event hadn't shown up and there were only two bouts to go. Strauss got dressed, left the building and came back in different clothes.

"I heard you needed a heavyweight," he said. The promoter looked at him and recognized him as the Mouse. "Get outta here," the promoter yelled. Most states provide for at least a 90-day rest after a knockout, to say nothing of 90 minutes.

"No, listen!" Strauss said. "I'm Bruce's twin brother, the Moose. He called me, said you needed somebody." Desperate, the promoter let him fight and Strauss was, naturally, knocked out. It stands as the all-time record: knocked out twice in one night.

It's like the time the old boxer was asked by a reporter if he'd ever broken his nose.

"Are you kiddin'?" he says. "My nose has been broken in four places."

"Wow," says the reporter. "Four places, huh?"

"Yeah," says the fighter. "New York, Atlantic City, Oakland and Las Vegas."

The average person has no idea what professional fighting is like. When Green Bay Packers lineman Tony Mandarich announced that he'd like to fight Mike Tyson not long ago, I nearly spit out my soup. What a giant joke. It reminded me of the time Jim Brown was in London for the Ali–Henry Cooper fight. He let it be known that he wanted to fight Ali for the heavyweight title. Ali called him and told him to meet him in Hyde Park. Once they were together, Ali stuck out that famous chin and told Brown to take his best shot at him, anything and everything he had. Brown wound up and Ali stepped in and started slapping him—*smack, smack, smack*—with his palm before Brown could even swing. Brown never even saw Ali's lightning hands. Brown never mentioned fighting again.

Maybe that's what makes boxing so colorful. Sane people *don't* fight. But very odd people do. People like Mitch (Blood) Green. Not a bad fighter at one time, Mitch gained repute for many achievements. For one, he went 10 rounds with Mike Tyson in 1986 and lost because, in his words, "I couldn't get motivated because of the money thing." Apparently, Green thought he hadn't been paid enough for the fight. But to my way of thinking, if you are in the ring with Tyson, you ought to be motivated because of the *surviving* thing. Mitch was also the guy who blocked Tyson's right fist with his eye at Dapper Dan's haberdashery in New York one night during the convenient shopping hours of 3 A.M. (Hey, Dan's was open.) Tyson broke his hand.

Mitch was once pulled over for driving through Harlem while watching a TV on his dashboard, intoxicated and accompanied by some angel dust and pills. He was hoping the arresting officers might grant him leniency. His license had only been suspended 54 times.

But the best Mitch (Blood) Green story is the time he drove his '79 Lincoln into a gas station in Queens, filled up and threatened the attendant, who ran off. Suddenly, Mitch was the only man working at the station. He got an idea. He began filling up cars and pocketing the money. Apparently he was about to forget to make change for a hundred-dollar bill from a cabbie when the cops pulled up. The cabbie tried to take his hundred back, only to get one of Mitch's fists in the face instead. Mitch was not voted Employee of the Month.

In the Mitch Green bout we telecast, he circled the ring so much that Ferdie and I were both getting dizzy. He also wanted to fight with a toothpick in his mouth, but the referee made him spit it out. Apparently, he was bent on becoming the U. L. Washington of the fight game.

Of course, if I had to trust my back to the fighters or the people who *run* the fighters, I'd pick the fighters. When Sonny Liston was just mauling people in the 1960s, he once smashed an opponent so bad it took a hundred stitches to repair the man's face. The poor man was his own worst enemy. As bloodied as he was, he kept coming back to face Liston. He would not call it quits. Afterwards, somebody asked Liston if his opponent was the bravest man he'd ever met. "No," said Liston with a scowl, "his manager was."

Don King and Bob Arum are two more people who are very brave with other people's careers. They are also two of the most manipulative people in sports. King uses racism to try to intimidate people. If you don't buy a fight from him, he immediately calls you a racist. At NBC, he used to go over the head of Kevin Monaghan, NBC's matchmaker, call up Arthur Watson, then president of NBC, and demand that Kevin be fired. To his credit, Watson would just say, "Sorry, Don, Kevin makes the fights. I can't help you."

Unfortunately, most of the time racial intimidation works. Nobody wants to be called a racist in the 1990s. Jarvis Astaire, the British fight promoter, always said that if King were white, he'd be ineffective. I think he's right.

Maybe the only guy who's worse is Arum. If you don't do business with Arum, he labels you the scum of the earth. He once crawled all over Ferdie and me for being "too objective" about the American fighters at the Seoul Olympics. He didn't like the fact that when a fighter stunk, we said he stunk. He complained vociferously that I was being too hard on the American boxers who weren't doing very well. What was I supposed to do? "This kid is a great prospect. When he regains consciousness, we'll interview him." (Of course, Arum is not the guy you want teaching your Ethics 100 class. This is the same man who once said, "Yesterday, I was lying. Today I'm telling the truth.")

We wondered why Arum should care so much about amateur fighters until a story broke that U.S. Olympic assistant coach Ken Adams had reached agreements on personal services contracts with two U.S. fighters—Kennedy McKinney and Ray Mercer—and Adams had allegedly signed a contract with Arum. So, in effect, Mercer, McKinney and Adams were already under Arum before the Olympics even began. No wonder during pre-fight background interviews, Adams kept telling us, "Mercer and McKinney, these are your best fighters." No matter who we brought up, he'd get back to those two. Hmmmm. Last I checked, Olympic boxing was supposed to be for amateurs.

Not that boxing ever made sense in the first place. It is the bloodiest and goriest of sports, yet the announcers always wear tuxedos. It is the only sport I know of where the athlete has no idea what the score is. In every other sport, an athlete knows where he stands. I'm down 40–love or two touchdowns or I'm five feet behind the guy. But in boxing, the judges mark on their secret cards and fighters don't know if they're 2 points behind or 10 ahead.

Integrity in boxing took the last train out a long time ago. Managers will hand us an information bio sheet that says their fighter has won 6 and lost 2, when our research shows him at 3 and 7. There's no way of knowing. Even their own press releases contradict other information within. Can you imagine this in any other sport? It would be like the Green Bay Packers playing the Kansas City Chiefs and the Packers claim they are 12 and 2 and someone else says, "No, that's not right. They're 8 and 4." It's senseless. Boxing is run by the managerial firm of Larry, Curly and Moe.

Life Is a Non-title Bout in Maracaibo

There's no single governing organization. There's no one central computer. There's no one national certifying body. The medical conditions are ridiculous. Ferdie, for instance, was adamant about not letting former Olympic gold medalist Sugar Ray Seales fight with only one good eye. Yet Seales fought. We learned afterward that Seales had memorized the eye chart to pass the physical despite being legally blind. We televised that bout—Seales vs. James Shuler. Seales lost. Ferdie also refused to do any of George Foreman's fights for Showtime because he felt Foreman should not be fighting. Ferdie refused even when he needed the money. And it was Ferdie who had it written into his contract that in any fight he did for NBC there must be an ambulance standing by. He had good reason. When he was calling the 1977 Durán-Leonard fight in Montreal with Brent Musburger, a fighter named Gaetan Hart defeated Cleveland Denny. While Ferdie was interviewing Hart, Denny collapsed. Ferdie tried to help him, but there was no ambulance to get him immediate help. Denny died in his arms.

Somebody has to help the fighters because fighters themselves won't. I've known boxers who have used one name in Minnesota, gotten knocked out, then driven over the weekend to Louisiana and been knocked out under a different name. All it would take is giving each fighter a computer ID number to stop that kind of thing, but nobody has done it. It's mumbo-jumbo organization. Fighters are risking their lives for peanuts. In 1992, we did a fight between Joey Gamache and Tony Lopez in Portland, Maine. On the undercard was the U.S. Olympic fighter Raoul Marquez, a big puncher, who would fight a pretty decent 9-and-2 right-hander. We wanted to show a few rounds of Marquez's fight, but the day of the fight, the promoter, a real character named Johnny Bos, dragged in this overblown lunch-meat welterweight to the weigh-in.

"What happened to the good opponent?" we asked.

"He's in jail," said Bos.

"Well, what's his bail?" we said.

"Five hundred dollars," said Bos.

"Well, let's bail him out. We need this guy."

"Nah," said Bos. "We were only giving him four hundred dollars for the fight to begin with."

Even at the highest levels, it's junk, from the WBC and WBA right down to the WBO, the NABF and, for a while there, the Continental Americas. Hey, there's a belt I *really* want to get hold of, the Continental Americas championship belt. Sounds like some sort of airline travel award.

And yet, because of its characters, it survives. Boxing is just made up of very different sorts of persons. We once hooked a wireless microphone to fight manager Lou Duva just before his fighter, Rocky Lockridge, was going to fight the painfully eccentric Livingstone Bramble. As Bramble walked by Duva wearing sunglasses in a darkened arena, you could hear Duva say, "We're going to knock those mother(bleep)ing sunglasses right off your face, you moron." And Lockridge did, in a stunning one-punch first-round knockout.

Naturally, one-punch first-round knockouts are about as much fun for a broadcaster as laryngitis. The longest two hours ever spent in broadcasting history was probably the day of the Marvis Frazier–Larry Holmes fight, a day filled with one-punch first-round knockouts on an NBC prime-time Friday-night special. Frazier, the son of Joe Frazier, was trying to put together some kind of career even though he really had no desire to be in the ring. He seemed to be your average nice kid who didn't want to hurt anybody. You got the feeling he just wanted to be a mortgage broker and leave it at that. But he was in the boxing game and he was going to put on a show. NBC's Dick Enberg tried to interview him in the dressing room before the fight and the entire family was barking at him. It was like a Ken-L-Ration ad.

The problem was, the preliminary fights were all first-round knockouts. Then Frazier came out and got knocked out by Holmes in the first round. We were left with about *an hour* to kill, which is the broadcasting equivalent of hell. Enberg interviewed the entire family again (worrying about distemper shots), while Ferdie and I recounted the history of modern boxing for the audience. It is the kind of night when I wished I had gone into piano like my mother wanted.

Life Is a Non-title Bout in Maracaibo

Then again, boxing has brought me some of the most unforgettable moments in my life. We were granted an interview with Muhammad Ali a couple of years ago on his 80-acre farm in Berrien Springs, Michigan. Ali hadn't given a decent interview in years and I knew why. One day in 1987, back when I was still doing sports for WNBC in New York, Ferdie and I were in Atlantic City for a big fight. Ferdie said, "Let's go by his hotel room and say hello." As soon as we went in, I knew it was a mistake. His hotel room was dark and he looked like a zombie, walking around aimlessly. He could barely talk. He recognized Ferdie and that was about it. The whole conversation was in slow motion. So I didn't hold much hope of getting anything good this time.

But I was wrong. We got lucky. We arrived there in the morning, when, apparently, he is more alert and the medication he needs for his Parkinson's hasn't set in yet. He actually provided very good answers. We were surprised. We let him look at a tape of one of his fights with Joe Frazier from the NBC's Greatest Fights Ever series and he said, "Boy, I was crazy," as though he were looking at someone else. "Was that me? Was I that fast?"

He was analytical. He praised Frazier, saying he couldn't have been Ali without Frazier. He said he lost to Frazier in that first fight because he didn't take it seriously enough. "I clowned too much," Ali said. "I didn't train like I should. I was too playful."

It all seemed to come back to him that morning. He even recounted all the things he'd contributed to boxing and it's a boatload: the rope-a-dope, the Ali shuffle, the double-clutch shuffle, the anchor punch, the ghetto rumble, the rabbit, the bear, the gorilla, the mummy, all the names, all the poems, all the memories, all the theatrics. Still, as the morning wore on and you saw his hands shake and you saw him shuffling around, you had to feel a little sad. I said, "Some people will watch this interview and compare the Ali of then to the Ali of today and say, 'What a shame.' Does that bother you?"

"No," Ali said. "Things change. I'm fatter now. I move slower. I get tired quicker. I can't go like I used to. I can't fight. And when I come back when I'm ninety years old, I'll look different. Mainly, my mind is still on top. Ask me a tough question."

"What do you do every day?" I said.

"Breathe," said Ali.

Then he started doing his old, bad magic tricks, including this awful levitation trick where he tries to make it appear as if he's rising out of the dust. Easily on the Bottom Ten of all-time magic tricks. One of his associates said it was very good. I said, "Don't quit your day job." He cracked up. I sensed he didn't want us to leave.

It reminded me of my first network broadcast fight in 1979: James Scott vs. Bunny Johnson from New Jersey's Rahway State Prison in 1979. Scott was a lifer. My color commentator was onetime heavyweight champion Ken Norton. We needed to interview Scott in prison before the fight. I remember Norton was so apprehensive about being behind prison walls that he took off all his jewelry. For Ken Norton, that's a lot of jewelry. He didn't want to show off and he didn't want to hear hoots from the prisoners. But once we got inside Scott's cell, Scott didn't want us to leave. He kept stalling, holding up the questions. Then he went around introducing us to his lovely friends. "This is Malcolm," Scott said. "He's in for murder." Apparently, Malcolm was part of a religious cult that enjoyed cutting the heads off people. Malcolm did an impression of me. It was brutal, but I gave him a *very high* rating.

Understandably we took criticism for televising fights from prison. Some people wanted to know since when does a man in prison get to continue his professional career? Are lifer tailors allowed to have their customers come by for alterations? What could we say? It was a good human-interest story. How could you resist the image? Here he was, in his boxing trunks, walking back through the prison, the barbed wire, the cinder-block walls. And I'd say, "So, for James Scott, it's another step toward the light heavyweight championship of the world. But for inmate 642789, it's back to Cellblock D, Ward 4, Cell 201." And the cell door would slam shut and we'd freeze on him and his boxing gloves. Chills.

At least we always knew where we could find him. One time we had a fighter just plain not show up. A guy named Ted Sanders was supposed to fight Alex Ramos in a rematch after Sanders's previous shocking eight-round TKO. Fine. We interviewed him and he told Ferdie it was going to be no fluke. Terrific. We built it up big, since it was the 200th broadcast of *Sportsworld,* NBC's weekend afternoon sports show. Unfortunately, three hours before the fight, nobody could find Mr. Sanders. He didn't weigh in. I expected him to show up anytime, saying something like he was kidnapped or held hostage on a bus or something bizarre, but he never did. It turned out he was unhappy with his hotel accommodations, so he left town. Perhaps the SpectraVision movies were not to his liking.

Sanders apparently lost his nerve at the last moment and I suppose I don't blame him. Boxing is the most brutal sport and yet, if you are around it enough, you become numb to it. It wasn't unusual for Ferdie and me to be sitting there at ringside during one of the preliminary matches, reading the newspaper and having some guy serve us our cheeseburger on a tray with silver salt and pepper shakers and linens. Do you have enough Grey Poupon? Why, yes, thank you. Meanwhile some poor sap is getting his pancreas beat out of him five feet in front of us. Pass the ketchup. One time we were eating and some guy's bloody mouthpiece landed right on my napkin. Ferdie pointed it out to me with a greasy french fry and laughed.

Ferdie is also not the sort of person you'd want to spend your last waking hour on earth with, yet I thought that might happen not just one time but two. The first was in the middle of England. We were doing the Tony Sibson–Frank Tate middleweight title bout. Times were very tough in that part of the country and there were a lot of hooligans in the crowd. Suddenly, I had this tickle in my throat. I started coughing. Then Ferdie started coughing. Then everybody at ringside started coughing. We looked up and some National Front guys—skinheads—were causing a ruckus in the stands. Tear gas had been released. It started getting very, very ugly. Then, luckily, the promoter brought Henry Cooper to the center-ring microphone. Cooper is the Brit who threw the lucky punch and knocked Ali down once upon a time. Cooper got up in the ring and said, "Please, please. The lads have trained so hard for this." Thank God for Henry Cooper. Things calmed down and we got out alive.

The second time was in Windsor, England. There was a bomb scare just before a title bout between Rocky Lockridge and Barry Michaels. I found this out because Mike Weisman, our producer, said into my earpiece, "Uh, Marv. There's been a bomb threat. We're leaving now. You and Ferdie can stay if you want to." Believe it or not, we didn't want to. We did a live shot on the sidewalk outside. I was standing in a trench coat in London reporting on possible bombs. I felt like Edward R. Murrow.

Those two things shook me up. I mean, I knew there was great resistance to Ferdie around the world, but I didn't think they'd go to *that* length.

Thanks, Marv. Thanks for nothing. Ever since you started announcing publicly whenever Connie and I leave Knicks games—
"The Poviches are making an *early* exit," you say—it has become a nightly event. And what do you think people say to us as we're walking out? "Way to go, Maury! Gonna go home and work on having a baby, right? Atta' way, Maury! Gotta get back home and get to it!"

When we *do* have a child, don't expect to be allowed anywhere *near* it.

—MAURY POVICH

7

Red Light Districts

The first hockey broadcast I ever did in my life looked like it would be my last. I was filling in for Jim Gordon on a Rangers game in Detroit at the old Olympia arena in 1963. I was a pup. I was a college student at NYU. The broadcast location was so antiquated, so discombobulated, that you actually had to look through a *periscope* which reflected off a *mirror* to see the scoreboard. Not only that, but the numbers you saw, since they were coming to you off a mirror, were backwards. That meant anytime you wanted to tell the listeners how much time was left in the game or in the penalty or who the penalty was called on or what the *score* was, you had to peer through a periscope like a German U-boat commander and try to read numbers backwards. The good news was, if I gave up broadcasting, I had enough experience that I could get a job painting letters on the front of ambulances.

I remember thinking after doing that game that it had gone so badly my career in hockey broadcasting was over. Instead, hockey became my first major league play-by-play opportunity. The broadcast rights to the Rangers went through a bunch of different hands, but ended up in 1965, strangely, at WHN, where they really didn't want them. The general manager, Roy Schwartz, wouldn't cross the street to see a sporting event if he had a free ticket in his pocket. He was into music formats and radio personalities. Naturally, I drove the man nuts until he let me do the Rangers. But not *all* of the Rangers.

Schwartz and I came to this most unusual compromise. I would broadcast only the last six minutes of the first and second periods and the entire third period of each game. It was like a theater showing you the first 10 minutes of a movie, then the middle 15 and the last 45. Still, it was all I could get. I took it. They'd be playing music or pumping some Bob and Ray skit for tomorrow morning's show, and all of a sudden it was "And now, let's go to Marv Albert at Chicago Stadium." Only what I'd do is cheat and tell them we were down to the last six minutes when there was really seven and a half. There, it's out. So sue.

Eventually, in 1966, the station relented and let me do entire games. And it's strange, but people ask me all the time, "When are you going to give up the hockey on radio?" I guess they think it's one job of my few dozen I don't really need. And I *know* I could use a night off once in a while in the throes of my busy season. But they don't understand. It's really my roots. It's the only *radio* I do and I think radio play-by-play keeps you sharp. And as soon as I'd quit, the Rangers would win the Stanley Cup, something they haven't accomplished since 1940.

Besides, how could I leave all the glamour? Like former Ranger Nick Fotiu locking me in the toilet on airplanes. Nick had this personal thing about airplane toilets. He did it to anybody who entered them. Thus, he taught an entire generation of New York Rangers to go before they took off.

And how could I leave guys like Rod Seiling, the ex-Ranger, who was so considerate that he once brought me a birthday present during his appearance on my WNBC radio talk show? After we finished, I opened it gratefully. It was a live rat. It got away.

I'd Love to But I Have a Game

It's still in Rockefeller Center somewhere, staying away from the commissary food like everybody else.

And where would I meet maniacs like former Rangers star Vic Hadfield, who used to quietly set fire to your newspaper as you were reading it? Vic also liked to call guys up, disguise his voice and tell them they'd been traded. "Hey, this is Slats Murphy from KWGN in Chicago," Vic would say. "What's your reaction to the trade?"

How could I give up the elegant Rangers fans, who, clear as a bell, chant "BULL-(BLEEP)! BULL-(BLEEP)!" directly behind me on the air when they don't like a call, thus leaving me to stammer, "The fans are voicing their displeasure at the referee's decision." One time, Bruce Beck of MSG Network was hosting a Rangers post-game show with Bobby Orr. The program included live call-ins. So this one caller gets on and says, "Bobby, you're the greatest hockey player ever." And Orr says, "Thank you very much." Then the caller says, "And, Bruce, you're the biggest (bleep) I ever saw." Poor Bruce was absolutely stuck. After the show, Bruce was in the hallway, visibly upset. Just then, Bob Gutkowski, president of Madison Square Garden, walks by and says, "Hey, Bruce, did you get my phone call?"

What about all the wonderful travel? The interesting work stations? Take, for instance, Philadelphia, where, at one time, 90 people were shrink-wrapped into a spot for 50. It was so crowded that as you were broadcasting, you were having to scoot your chair up and back so people can get by. *And here's the face-off . . . certainly . . . Rangers drop it into the corner . . . oh, my pleasure . . . there's a shot and . . . yes, I'm fine, fine . . . he scooooooooores!*

And how could I leave the Sutter brothers, the traveling broadcast nightmare? Have you ever tried to keep track of every Sutter brother? I'm not sure Mrs. Sutter can do it, much less the broadcasters. I mean, on radio, you can't just say, "Sutter across the blue line." You have to say *which* Sutter across the blue line. And there are, at last count, 47 Sutters in the NHL. Same with the Hunter brothers, especially when they both played for the Caps. I remember wishing one of the Hunter brothers, just for the Rangers games, would go down with sinus congestion. Nothing serious.

The longest hour of my life occurred in hockey. In 1976, I helped broadcast the Philadelphia Flyers' series of games with the Soviet National Hockey team. It was hard to say which team America hated most—the Soviets or the Flyers. Philadelphia was the murderous Broad Street Bullies and they weren't going to suddenly start sitting back and eating quiche for the Russians. Halfway into the game, the Flyers brutalized a Soviet skater and no penalty was called. The Soviets were incensed—so incensed they took their players off the ice. And they didn't come back for an hour. Have you ever tried to fill on television *for an hour?* By about 55 minutes, Gene Hart (the radio voice of the Flyers) and I were reminiscing about certain bowls of borscht we'd had in the past.

Oh, hockey has been a festival of fun. Last year, for a Rangers game with the Detroit Red Wings, my color partner Sal (Red Light) Messina and I had to do almost an entire game *on the phone.* It happened. There was some kind of scheduling mix-up and suddenly both of us realized that we had neither an engineer nor a broadcast console at our broadcast location. What could we do? We winged it. Howie Rose, who usually shares Rangers play-by-play duty with me, was in the studio in Astoria, Queens, and did the play-by-play from there watching a television. Red Light did color commentary from a phone in the press room watching the game on TV. Like a lot of American homemakers, I stayed and waited for the telephone installation man to come.

Eventually, he did come and install two phone lines in our booth, which enabled Sal and me to do the rest of the game talking into telephones. We really never missed a thing, except the broadcast quality was about that of Radio Free Antarctica. Still, there was an advantage to doing a game on the telephone. During commercials, Sal was able to make personal calls.

That had never happened to me in my life before, but it's already happened to my son, Kenny. He was doing play-by-play for the Washington Capitals' farm team, the Baltimore Skipjacks, when, one night, the engineering equipment failed. They had to do the entire game through *one* phone. Kenny would do some action, then hand the phone to his color analyst, Dave Starman, who would talk until it was time for more play-by-play. At one point in the third period, Starman started losing his sanity a little bit. He handed the phone to Kenny and said, "Here, it's for you." Naturally, the next day at the radio station, somebody came up to Kenny and said, quite seriously, "Boy, the broadcast sounded *really* clear last night."

Can I mention here that Kenny scored the first goal in the history of the NYU hockey club? Of course I can. It's my book. Kenny loves hockey the way I love basketball. Kenny is a good kid. It's simply that there are a few things about him that just aren't *right*. For instance, from the time he was a child, he was a Vancouver Canucks fan. Here he was, a New Yorker. His father was the radio voice of the New York Rangers. He regularly came to the Rangers games. He knew many of the Rangers players personally, and yet he insisted on being a Canucks fan. He even wore a Canucks jersey as a boy to a Rangers' Christmas party one year. I told Brad Park he had my permission to fore-check him into the eggnog.

You have to be a little skewed to like minor league hockey as much as Kenny did. They traveled mostly by bus, but even their rare airplane trips—to wonderful spots like the Canadian Maritimes—were hell. That's because the Skipjacks had an unwritten code for airplane trips: Players must wear coat and tie. Unfortunately, the players had an unwritten code too: Anybody who falls asleep would have their tie cut off. And so here you had a group of guys on a hellish flight schedule—from Baltimore to Boston to Nova Scotia—all eyeing each other warily and trying to get sleep out of one eye. Wonderful for team performance.

The Skipjacks had one of the few black players in hockey on that team when Kenny was part of it—Reggie Savage, who is now with Quebec. He is the adopted son of white parents from Montreal. As such, he happens to have a blond, blue-eyed sister. When the Skipjacks joined the Washington Capitals for camp in Lake Placid, New York, one fall, a bunch of the veterans were checking out the beautiful blond sitting in the stands at practice.

Nothing unusual in that, except Reggie started to get a little annoyed. "Hey," he said, "watch out now. That's my sister." Every puck, skate, drill and whistle in the place stopped dead.

My sidekick Red Light is very big in minor league hockey circles. Sal Messina was one of the most famous goalies in the history of the Long Island Ducks, not to mention the Philadelphia Ramblers. He was also the backup goaltender for a U.S. national team in 1963, for whom he had the pleasure of traveling to Moscow during the height of the Cold War. He often reminds me how difficult it was to walk the streets with three guys toting machine guns watching your every step. I think he was emotionally affected by that trip. To this day, every now and then, Sal will take off his shoe and pound it on the table to get a waitress's attention.

Sal has this thing about never missing a game. He could be shot walking over to the Garden, stabbed on the way up the escalator, mugged walking down the hallway and he would still crawl to the booth, bloody, and put on the headphones. If he's got a cold, flu, fever, sore throat, diphtheria, doesn't matter, Sal always comes to the game, where he is kind enough to give me or Howie Rose whatever current disease he is harboring.

Somehow, in his mind, Sal fancies himself as the Lou Gehrig of hockey broadcasting. It seems he told a reporter that he'd made 1,300 straight games without missing. I believe Sal took too many shots in the mask during Long Island Ducks shooting practice. What he doesn't tell them is that he has a streak going of 1,300 straight games *he can get to*. He figures if he tells us way in advance that he's going to miss a game, then it doesn't count against his streak. I'm pretty sure that's the way Gehrig's streak worked, don't you? *Uh, fellas. I've got a dentist appointment the day of that Boston doubleheader. I'll pick up the streak when I get back.*

I think Sal's fixation on making it to every game—or saying he has—stems from his years as the backup goaltender for the Rangers in 1963 and 1964. It is from those years that Sal's greatest hockey moment sprang: The night he *almost* was inserted into a regular-season game. The Rangers' Jacques Plante, seven-time winner of the Vezina Trophy as best NHL goaltender, was sick for a game in Montreal against the venerable Canadiens. They told Sal at about two that afternoon and his stomach was in pretzels the rest of the day. Tragically, moments before the teams were to take the ice, Plante got better. The Rangers won 3–1. Sal never did get in an NHL game. To this day, perhaps to heal the inner scars, Sal always tries to interview the backup goalie between periods.

I gave Sal his nickname Red Light in honor of the many glorious goals he gave up. I always felt a little sorry for goalies anyway. I played goalie in roller hockey. My brother Al was one. It's a cruel job. Plante himself described it best: "How would you like it if you were sitting in your office and you made one little mistake and suddenly a big red light went on and 18,000 people jumped up and started screaming at you, calling you a bum and an imbecile and throwing garbage at you. That's what it's like when you play goal in the NHL."

Actually, the original Red Light was a goaltender for the Rangers by the name of Dunc Wilson. Dunc was a real character, a party guy. One night in Toronto, Dunc gave up a few goals and the Toronto fans started calling him Red Light. So Hugh Delano, the hockey writer for the New York *Post,* wrote about it. The next day, Dunc came up to Hugh in a panic. "Hugh, don't put that stuff in the paper! My wife will think I'm hanging out in the wrong parts of town!"

Sal is sort of the Albert family mascot. He has now done color for Al, Steve, Kenny and me. And I think I speak for all of us when I say, we are all *very* tired of him. One time, Sal said, "Well, Marv, looking at the replay, he had his back legs pulled out from under him, definitely a penalty." Back legs? What was he, Secretariat?

The first hockey color man I worked with was Bill (the Big Whistle) Chadwick, the popular Hall of Fame referee. Big Whistle was the guy who devised the signals for penalties in hockey. Ironically, Big Whistle was blind in one eye. Also ironically, he was constantly criticizing the refs. Anything went wrong, he blamed the refs.

I don't think the refereeing is what's kept the NHL behind the other major sports in this country. Basically, it's a sport that doesn't play well on television. It's the opposite of football. You need to be there to really enjoy it. In football, you'll probably enjoy it more if you're sitting at home because of the benefit of replays. It doesn't help either that there are so many Europeans in the NHL. It's like the NASL on skates. I'm not sure kids can relate to Alexei Zhitnik or Igor Ulanov. Alexei Zhitnik sounds like something you could get your mouth washed out with soap for saying.

If the NHL wanted to eliminate fighting, they could. Tomorrow. In the NBA, you throw a punch, you're out of the game. Same in the NFL. But the owners think the fans like the feeling that anything can happen at any time. The problem is, there is so *much* posturing and fighting, it loses its spontaneity. I once saw the Flyers get into a fight before the officials were even on the ice. Rugged defenseman Neil Sheehy, a Harvard grad, actually took boxing lessons and studied fight videotapes to improve his fighting technique. Do you think Julio Cesar Chavez studies power-play tapes? There are even fans now who collect hockey fight footage. *I'll trade my cool Dave Semenko knockout tape for your Tie Domi head-butt victory.*

Perhaps all my years calling hockey fights has helped my boxing blow-by-blow techniques on NBC. In fact, the most gruesome fight I ever saw was not on canvas but on ice. It involved a Ranger way back when by the name of Orland Kurtenbach, a real Clint Eastwood type—a tough, silent guy who would be the last man on earth you would want to, say, short-sheet. The Rangers were in Detroit—I was looking through the periscope at the scoreboard—and suddenly Kurtenbach became riled up about something the Red Wings' Bert Marshall had done. Kurtenbach's gloves came flying off. Only, this time, under the gloves, he was wearing white skintight rubber gloves. He threw the most incredible one-two combination I've ever seen and it was over. No Detroit player came to Marshall's rescue. No Detroit player had time. When Kurtenbach stepped away, Marshall was lying on the ice, unconscious. They had to remove him on a stretcher. Looking back on it, I think Marshall was using the Vampire Johnson defense.

Later, when the team was a legitimate contender and loaded with stars like Rod Gilbert, Brad Park, Vic Hadfield and Jean Ratelle, they could have used a guy like Kurtenbach. Some fans felt that it always hurt the Rangers that Emile Francis, the Rangers' coach and general manager, didn't believe in going out and acquiring enforcers and goons. I specifically remember the Rangers losing the seventh game of the 1974 playoff semifinal series to the Flyers because they sat and watched Dave Schultz beat the bejeebers out of Dale Rolfe. Nobody would step in. The Rangers said later that the NHL's "third-man rule," in which the third man to enter a fight gets thrown out of the game, kept them away. But it would have been worth it. Schultz beat him to a pulp in front of the entire Rangers team. That the Rangers let him do it basically symbolized their fear of the Flyers.

Since 1940, the Rangers have made two appearances in the Stanley Cup finals and lost both times. But the year I thought they actually might win was in 1971, especially after the unforgettable sixth game of the Stanley Cup semifinals with the Chicago Black Hawks. I can't forget it because of my own, ahem, personal condition that night.

I hadn't gone to the bathroom the entire game and was planning on doing it immediately after the game was over. The only problem was, the game went into overtime. I couldn't leave the broadcast table because I'd never make it back in time. I was in trouble. Then it went into double overtime. I was dying. Suddenly, I realized we were going into triple overtime. That's when somebody gave me a bottle and I did it in there. And there you have it, ladies and gentlemen, another . . . (kettle drums) Great Moment in Broadcast History.

I also remember that night because we had a babysitter named Michael Levinson home with three-year-old Kenny. I'd never done this before and never since, but along about the third overtime I sent out a personal message to my house. "Michael," I said, "we'll be home a little late tonight."

Finally, the Rangers' Pete Stemkowski scored a goal at 11:29

of the third overtime to tie the series at three games each. It was one of the most dramatic series I ever saw, considering that was the third overtime game of the series (Stemkowski had won Game 1 with a goal in overtime too). It was a chilling moment. And I remember the Big Whistle saying, "There's no stopping this Rangers club after an overtime victory like that!"

The next night, they were eliminated.

Personally, I blamed the refs.

There's no question that to the real Albert aficionado the single greatest moment in Marv's career is not Willis Reed's two baskets, not the call of the Dream Team's Olympics, not Jordan's right-to-left-hand switch in Game 2 against the Lakers, not Eddie Giacomin's, "kick save and a beauty," not some vicious right hand of John (the Beast) Mugabi, not his searing interviews with Whitey Herzog or Jim Rice or Darryl Dawkins, but rather the following moment:

Game 3, NBA playoffs. Bulls at Knicks. Saturday-afternoon game. Marv Albert and Mike Fratello. They come out of a commercial with a bumper. It's a shot of the street outside the Garden. In the background, the marquee reads: "Bulls vs. Knicks." In the foreground, there is a bulldog, fully dressed in a sport coat and a hat. There is a cigarette dangling from the bulldog's lips. They go back inside the Garden, two or three seconds go by, and then Marv utters the following:

"Mike, always *so* troubling when a dog smokes."

—Bob Costas

8

Why I Hate Chris Evert

Race-car drivers like to hear wreck stories. Death-row inmates love a good gas-chamber joke. And sports announcers relish the occasional on-air disaster of Godzilla proportions.

NBC's Bob Costas, slightly demented that he is, tells one of the best. It happened one night on KMOX in St. Louis, where Costas began his broadcasting career and now lives. It was a sleepy Wednesday-night Cardinals game. Jack Buck, Mike Shannon and Bob Starr were in the booth. It was Dairy Day at the ballpark. It was the fourth inning and the public relations guy for the Greater Dairy Farmers Association of Missouri or some such place came into the booth in the fourth inning. Walking in with him was a gorgeous, well-endowed, bikini'd, blond young woman in high heels wearing a sash that read: "Miss Cheesecake." Miss Cheesecake brought three cheesecakes with her. She sashayed down the stairs to where the announcers sat and put a cheesecake in front of each one of them. There was a bit of a break in the action and

Jack Buck said to Bob Starr, "Hey, Bob, whaddya think about Miss Cheesecake?"

Starr thought Buck asked, "Whaddya think about *this* cheesecake?" So Bob Starr answered, "I'll tell you something, Jack. I'd like a piece of that *right now.*"

Costas once had a beauty himself doing a 1985 NBC Baseball Game of the Week. Tony Kubek was his color man. It was a Toronto game and on the screen came a shot of Tommy John, the ex-New York Yankees pitcher. The Blue Jays had just signed him, but John was on a rehab assignment and was only charting pitches. "Tony, there's Tommy John, twenty-game winner in both leagues for the Yankees and the Dodgers," Costas said. "The Jays think they'll have him in the starting rotation, but not soon enough. He'll be pissing in Appleton until then." It immediately came to Costas what he had said. *"Pitching* in Appleton," he added quickly. There was a pause. "Come to think of it," said Costas. "If he stays in Appleton long enough, he'll probably do both."

These are the kinds of things that make you wake up at 3:30 in the morning in a cold sweat. There was the time Yankees broadcaster Phil Rizzuto opened a game by saying cheerfully, "Hi, everybody, I'm Bill White." Upon which, his color commentator, Bill White, said, "No, Phil, that's me."

In New York, we are lucky to have Ralph Kiner, broadcaster for the New York Mets. Kiner is a good enough broadcaster, it's just that every now and then his tongue gets going too fast for his teeth. One night, Kiner was in the booth when the batter smashed a long drive deep into the outfield. "It's gone!" Kiner said, then added, "Nope. He caught it."

Kiner once called his color man, Tim McCarver, "Tim MacArthur" and once referred to the Charlotte Hornets as the Charlotte Harlots. He used to do a post-game interview for Martin Paints, and every now and again he'd get the guest name confused with the product. When longtime manager Gene Mauch came on one night, for instance, Kiner said, "My guest tonight, of course, Gene Martin."

One night, after a Mets win over the Houston Astros, he was

explaining why reliever Jesse Orosco was not credited with a save. "He did not have, he did not pitch three innings, and he came in without the, ah, the on-deck batter, being a batter that he would face in, ah, his next approach to pitching to the hitter."

I think that pretty much cleared it up for everybody.

Nowadays, with satellite telecasts, broadcasters can get themselves in new, improved kinds of trouble. When you are doing a satellite game, which is quite often, you have to remember that people who have satellite dishes stay with the feed when the regular cable subscribers go to a commercial. That means they can hear *anything* you say. One time, Hot Rod Hundley, the voice of the Utah Jazz, was just starting up with a new sidekick, Frank Layden. It was halftime in the Boston Garden. The live feed was being piped into the Celtics locker room. During a commercial, Layden spots a familiar figure in the stands.

"Rod, look at that sonuvabitch Auerbach," Layden said.

"Frank, be careful," said Hundley, "we're on satellite. Anyone taking our feed can hear what you're saying."

Layden either didn't understand what Hundley meant or didn't care, because he kept on. "Satellite, schmatellite, I'd like to take that cigar of Red's and shove it up his (bleep)."

"For God's sake, Frank," said Hundley. "It's still lit."

On Raycom Sports one night, analyst Dave Rowe was watching Syracuse running back David Walker catch a controversial touchdown against USC. As Walker scored, he brushed the pylon in the corner of the end zone. "He hit the pontoon," Rowe said. "If he hits the pontoon, it's a touchdown." It's an old Coast Guard rule.

Of course, I don't know why I have to limit this to brilliant things announcers say. Not all athletes that announcers interview are exactly Rhodes scholars. Somebody asked Olympic boxer Henry Tillman, a native of Los Angeles, how far he lived from the L.A. Sports Arena, site of the Olympic boxing venue. "Oh, about three and a half to four miles," Tillman said, "depending on traffic."

Baltimore manager Earl Weaver once was having a difficult time explaining why so many home runs were being hit in Tiger

Stadium. "Hey, I'm not a meteorologist or a gynecologist or anything like that."

When William (the Fridge) Perry was at Clemson, a reporter came to him to ask him about the news that Clemson had just been put on two-year TV and bowl probation. "How's that affect you, Fridge?" the guy asked.

"Well," said Perry, "the bowl thing isn't so bad. But what makes it hard is that we can't watch television for two years."

Everybody tells Yogi Berra stories, but I like to think of myself as a connoisseur. After Johnny Bench broke Berra's record for most home runs by a catcher, Yogi sent him a telegram. It read: "Congratulations on breaking my record last night. I always thought the record would stand until it was broken."

Then there was the time Yogi was invited to the White House for a state dinner. When he got home, he was disappointed. "I thought they said *steak* dinner."

Yogi was the featured guest on a radio talk show. The host began by saying, "Yogi, if you don't mind, when we go on, I'd like to play 'free association' with you on the air. I'll say a name and you say the first thing that comes to your mind, O.K.?"

So Yogi says, "O.K."

When the show started, the host went right into it. "We've got Yogi Berra of the New York Yankees here and he and I are going to do some free-associating. I'm going to say a name and Yogi's going to say the first thing that pops into his mind. O.K., Yogi, ready?

"Ready," Yogi says.

"Mickey Mantle."

"What about him?"

At least the radio man had proof that he had the real Yogi in front of him. One time color commentator Cal Ramsey was working a Knick telecast and wasn't so lucky. He told his listeners, "At halftime we'll be talking with National League All-Star Joe Morgan." When he came back, he did a quick in-person interview with Morgan and it all seemed to go fine. They said goodbye. People began calling in from everywhere. That *wasn't* Joe Morgan. It was an imposter. Ramsey had been duped.

Worse things have happened to an announcer. Johnny Most, the legendary play-by-play man for the Boston Celtics, used to smoke while he worked. During one broadcast he got a bit excited and didn't realize the cigarette he'd been smoking had dropped down into his lap. He carried on for a while, smelled something burning and realized it was none other than himself. To his credit, he did the call of it on the air.

Most had another weird thing happen to him. In his later years, he'd been having trouble with his hearing and, after about a year, went to see a doctor about it. The doctor looked in his ear and saw something strange. He did a little more probing and finally pulled out the foreign object. It was the little rubber plug that fits over a broadcaster's earpiece. Somehow it had come off and, as they say in golf, plugged.

Live broadcasts offer all sorts of unforeseen hazards. Butch Beard, the former NBA guard, was my television color man for a while with the Knicks. On the road, after we rehearsed the opening, it was our little ritual to go into the Knicks locker room while they were in their warm-ups and do some last-second vanity stuff—check the mirror, a little more pancake, whatever. One night, we were at the old Milwaukee Mecca. We went into the locker room, did our stuff and then started to leave. We had about five minutes to airtime. As we pushed the door to leave, it didn't budge. The door was locked. Somebody had locked it, figuring, perhaps, that it was easier to guard the Knicks' stuff that way. Whatever the reason was, we were very definitely locked in with only minutes to airtime. We started banging on the door, trying to get out. We realized the team wasn't coming back in there. They were warming up and then going straight to the bench for the game. It was quite conceivable that we were going to miss the start of the game. Or, for that matter, the game itself. Finally, one minute before airtime, our hands bruised from pounding, a cop heard us banging and opened the door. We ran to the table just as the Knicks were being introduced. The Knicks had a lot of suspicious smirks on their faces. I have only three words to say to the perpetrator: Nair in jock.

Speaking of disasters, my co-author on this book, Rick Reilly of *Sports Illustrated,* did one of the dumbest things I've ever seen on the air. He was getting ready to be interviewed live on ESPN from his living room. He had his earpiece in his ear and could hear the voice from ESPN saying, "O.K., relax a couple minutes. We'll be coming to you soon." Well, relaxing sounded pretty good to him since he was a little nervous. One way he liked to relax was to do deep-breathing exercises. You know, *big* breath in, hold it, *big* breath out. One inhale and exhale would take him at least twenty seconds and make him look like he was about to go into deep fits of yoga. Well, while he was doing this, the line to his earpiece went out without his knowing it. So when ESPN came to him live and asked their first question, all they saw him doing was *big* breath in, *big* breath out. At first, it seemed as if maybe Reilly was contemplating the question slowly and surely and about to give the most well-thought-out answer in the history of broadcast interviewing. But when he started to take another *big* breath in, the announcers realized he couldn't hear them. "Well, we know he's breathing," said the ESPN announcer. Eventually, they came back to him and it worked, but is that the stupidest thing you've ever . . . (Rest of paragraph lost in text preparation.)

There are bad traps to get in while you're *on* the air too. Dick Enberg, the longtime NBC announcer, had to do a UCLA-Oregon game years ago in which UCLA moved ahead 10–2 in the first minute and simply held the ball the rest of the game just to avoid an awful embarrassment for Oregon. There was no 45-second college clock then. It was great for UCLA's relationship with Oregon, but it left poor Dick holding a bomb. He had nothing to call. UCLA just held it and the Ducks let them hold it. Dick ran through every note he had, every stat, every fact, every observation about the game, and he still had much time to kill. It had been raining, and, at that time, the movie *Butch Cassidy and the Sundance Kid* was just out. So Enberg started humming the theme song from it, "Raindrops Keep Falling on My Head."

People gave him such a hard time about it that during his next game on the air, UCLA vs. Oregon State, Dick said he'd *sing* "Raindrops" at midcourt at Pauley Pavilion if and when UCLA clinched the conference title. Well, that tore the cover off it. Every game after that, the UCLA band would strike up "Raindrops" to mark the moment when the Bruins had sewn up a game. Eventually, they won the title. Dick was at the game. There was no getting out of it. He stalled for half an hour hoping people would leave, but nobody did. At last, he got to the mike and delivered absolutely the worst performance in the history of song. They say three floors of window were broken in the nearby physics hall. "I tried to tell them," Enberg said afterwards. "I can't sing."

I've never heard Costas sing on the air, but I think I've seen him do everything else, including play-by-play for dogsled, elevator and taxicab races on *Late Night with David Letterman*. In fact, Costas got off one of the greatest lines in the history of late-night TV during a baby race. It was the third anniversary of *Late Night* and the writers got this idea to see if a baby would be born during the taping of the show. They were going to call it the Late Night Baby and give it all kinds of incredible benefits in perpetuity. So they stationed Costas at a New York hospital and they kept checking in with him.

"Dave, behind this door, six women are actually in labor," Costas said in his opening. "In a little while, we'll be back with all the pre- and post-natal action." Unfortunately, there would be no fetus to greet us. Time after time, they checked in with Bob, but he had no baby to present. Finally, Letterman told the doctors and nurses to eat all the cake and ice cream and have the party anyway. The doctors were smoking the cigars and the nurses were blowing the noisemakers and everybody was feeding on the goodies when they checked in with Costas one last time.

"I'm afraid there is still no baby," Costas said amid the merriment. "But the party continues apace." He looked over his shoulder at the doctors and nurses carrying on and then he said, "Meanwhile, the plaintive cries of desperately ill men and women go unheeded."

Costas once asked me to name every partner I've ever worked with and I told him it wasn't many. Only, alphabetically, Kenny Albert, John Andariese, Red Auerbach, Elgin Baylor, Butch

Beard, Carl Braun, Lou Carnesecca, Eddie Donovan, Mike Fratello, Walt Frazier, Elliott Gould, Steve Grote, Richie Guerin, Rod Hundley, Phil Jackson, Magic Johnson, Steve Jones, Toby Knight, Jerry Lucas, Al McGuire, Tom Penders, Ron Perry, Digger Phelps, Cal Ramsey, Willis Reed and Bucky Waters in basketball; John Brodie, Chip Cipolla, Len Dawson, Bob Griese, Mike Hafner, Sam Huff, Jimmy Johnson, Marv Levy, Dick Lynch, Paul Maguire, Joe Namath, Vic Obeck, Merlin Olsen, Bill Parcells, Ed Podolak, Dave Rowe, Bob Trumpy and Jim Turner for football; Don Awrey, Curt Bennett, Bill (the Big Whistle) Chadwick, Bill Clement, John Davidson, Phil Esposito, Ron Greschner, Gene Hart, Steve Jensen, Dan Kelly, Pierre Larouche, Dave Maloney, Sal (Red Light) Messina, Stan Mikita, Chris Nilan, Denis Potvin, Chico Resch, Tim Ryan, Gene Stuart and Garry Unger for hockey; Bobby Czyz, Don Dunphy, Ray Leonard, Larry Merchant, Ken Norton, Ferdie Pacheco, Art Rust, Jr., and Rollie Schwartz for boxing; Bob Costas, Joe Morgan, Don Sutton, Mike Schmidt, Bobby Valentine and Maury Wills for baseball. Looking at that list makes me realize one obvious thing: I need a better agent.

One guy I remember well is Brodie. He was *the* most laid-back man in the history of California. Most professional games I do, I arrive at the site of the game on Friday night. Both the play-by-play man and the color analyst try to do as much preparation from home as they can—looking at tapes, reading clips, studying press guides—and then meet up at the site. But once in a while, we'd each leave from our respective homes first thing Saturday morning. Well, early one Saturday morning, I was on my way out the door for one of these trips and the phone rang. It was my color man, Brodie.

"Hello, Marv?"

"Hi, John."

"How are you?"

"Just fine, John."

"Say, Marv, do you mind telling me one thing?"

"Sure, John."

"Which game are we doing this week?"

Is it any wonder color analysts are the bane of my existence? One time, Butch Beard had two guys in the top row hold up a sign that said, "Marv Albert Fan Club." Both guys were asleep.

Maybe because I like to poke fun at my color guys, people in the business seem to relish it when I get hammered. For instance, I did the 6 and 11 o'clock sports for 13 years on NBC-TV, and sometimes, in the rush to get back from a Rangers game or a Knicks game at the Garden, the technical aspects of the broadcast wouldn't go exactly as scripted, much to the unending amusement of the people not involved. One night I started the sports with an interview with pitcher Ed Halicki of the Giants, who had blanked the Mets that afternoon. "Here's what Big Ed had to say about it," I said. Up came the tape . . . of Chris Evert discussing that weekend's World Team Tennis match.

The camera came back to me. Now, the idea here is to try *not* to look desperate. Your mind is racing. You're wondering what went wrong. You want to kill everybody in sight. You see, through your peripheral vision, weatherman Frank Field and news anchor Chuck Scarborough laughing like hyenas, loving every minute of your torture. Basically, if you had a pistol, you'd be doing some serious time.

Still, you carry on. 'Folks," I said. "Big Ed Halicki has *really* changed." Nevertheless, I persevered. I went on with the sportscast and then said, *"Now* we'll hear what Chris Evert has to say about tomorrow's World Team Tennis match." This time nothing came up at all. Back to me, looking like an idiot. Nevertheless, I persevered. I began reading the baseball scores and every single one of them came up wrong on the screen. The camera came back to me. Unfortunately, I didn't know this and, as I was reading the scores, the camera was focused on the top of my head. I finally looked up and realized I had been on the air for a good thirty seconds.

I stopped persevering. "Well, folks, it's been one of those memorable nights in sports. Thank you and good night."

Scarborough was having a grand old time with my troubles. "Marv," he said, "all of us took a vote and we'd like you to try for the Chris Evert interview again." So we did. It came up in the middle.

At times, doing live local newscasts is one death-defying moment after another and having Dr. Frank Field as our weatherman on those newscasts didn't help. He was a well-respected weatherman and science reporter, true, but what people didn't realize was that Frank was slightly skewed. He was known for his dinner-time health reports in which he would show live heart surgery and the occasional kidney transplant. We had a saying around the newsroom, "If you want to lose weight, turn on Frank Field. You won't be able to eat your dinner."

Field loved to try and make you break up. One time anchorman Tom Snyder was reading a serious piece about thousands of ducks frozen in the ice in a lake in the South. Suddenly, Snyder noticed Frank off to the side. Frank started making duck noises, just loud enough for Snyder to hear. Very, very *good* duck noises. Snyder was trying not to break up, but he was in tears. I'm sure he got a few hundred letters saying, "How can you be so *insensitive* to ducks!"

Frank's karma came back to get him, though. One week, he was doing the network's morning *Today* show *and* the 6 and 11 P.M. weather. That meant getting up at 4 A.M. and working until midnight. One day during that stretch, he'd worked all day on a package for the 6 o'clock newscast that night, did his weather and finally had a minute to rest before he had to start working on the 11. He put his head back in a chair offstage and fell asleep. There was still time left in the newscast when Scarborough saw him and had the cameras turned on him. "Folks," Scarborough said, "I want to show you how Frank Field prepares his weather reports." Frank never even woke up. Personally, I'd never seen Frank show so much on-air charisma.

One Mother's Day, Frank was doing the weather in New York. It was an inclement Mother's Day, rainy, cold and windy, so when the anchor, Jim Hartz, threw it to Frank, he said, "Now, here's the man responsible for this dreadful day, Frank Field." So Frank takes over and the first thing he says is "I'm sorry about the weather, you mothers out there."

The place went to pieces. Frank had no idea what was wrong. He checked his fly. That wasn't it. He tried to carry on while his stage crew was in tears. Finally, he went to a commercial. When it was clear, he asked, "What'd I say?"

"Frank," said his stage manager. "You used half a word."

One last Frank story: He was going to shoot the opening of the Philharmonic at Central Park for a little weather feature one day and convinced me to accompany him. Frank sat me down with the four lady harpists in the orchestra and put one of their harps in my hands. I was in that shot. Then he sat me with the horn section. I was in that shot. Then in the string section. Then the drums. So when the little piece ran during the weather, I was in *every* section of the orchestra. Only Frank played it totally straight. Never said a thing about me. Just: "A beautiful day in Central Park today for the opening of the Philharmonic's outdoor season." Then he threw it to me for sports. I nearly lost it. The switchboard lit up. People couldn't believe what they'd seen. "Hey! That guy in the trombone section looked *just like* Marv Albert!"

Was he playing "Malagueña"?

Even before I met Marv I knew a great way to drive him nuts. On the first limo ride we ever took together, we were in Detroit and I said, "Do you know anything about basketball?" He just sort of rolled his eyes. So I then said, "O.K., name me a Celtic guard from 1968. Jewish." It drove him crazy. He could not get it. Here's this walking computer of information and I ask him a simple trivia question and he's stuck. Even right up to game time, he was pacing the booth trying to think of it. Here I am trying to make my network color-man debut and he's pacing the booth trying to think of it. He never did get it and I refuse to tell him. But, seeing as how this is his book, I'll tell him now.

Ricky Weitzman.

Man knows nothing about basketball.

—BILL PARCELLS

9

The Wyoming State Porcupines

And now for the only priest-punching story I know.

My longtime color analyst on NBC college games, Bucky Waters, was doing a game at Niagara, a Catholic university, for their game against St. John's. Not exactly Duke-UCLA, but good enough. Now, most days, Bucky is a true scholar and gentleman. He is a vice-chancellor at Duke University and was formerly the head basketball coach at both Duke and West Virginia. He still works as a color commentator on college games for Madison Square Garden Network and on ACC games. For 15 years, he and I traveled the country for NBC trying to hear each other talk while college bands played, cheerleaders shrieked and fans with painted faces tried to scream holes into the backs of our skulls. If you let it, it can get to you. I'm afraid this is what happened to Bucky.

At halftime for this particular game, Bucky was scheduled to interview one of the priests from the administration of Niagara.

I'd Love to But I Have a Game

The priest even gave Bucky about six or seven questions before-hand. "These are the questions I'd like you to ask me," the priest said, politely. "In that order." The questions were innocuous lay-ups. Fine. But then the priest comes back and says, "I'd like to change the order of the questions. I want number three to be number one." Fine.

So now it's halftime and Bucky is standing out on the floor with the priest and they throw it to him and Bucky introduces the priest and he asks Question No. 3 first: "Father, what's unique about Niagara?" Well, suddenly the priest's nostrils distend, his pupils dilate, and he begins salivating over his lower lip. "Well, I'll *tell* you what's unique about Niagara. *We're not for sale!*" Whereupon, he launches into a soliloquy about Catholic educa-tion and government subsidies and next thing you know he's deep into this huge New York controversy about public schools vs. parochial. *"And another thing! Niagara will never bow down to the . . ."* And on and on. The man is very close to incoherent. By this time, the priest has both hands around Bucky's micro-phone. In broadcast interviewing, there is one cardinal rule: Never Let Go of Your Microphone. If you let go, you might never get it back and that can only end in disaster. In Bucky's ear, the guys in the truck were saying, "Bucky, if you let go of that microphone, you're fired." So by now there's four hands on the mike and the priest is still shouting.

"Niagara will *not* take any state money!" The priest is a bruiser and he's winning the microphone wrestling contest. He has moved the microphone close enough to his face that his lips are inches from it. From the truck, a voice tells Bucky, "If he eats it, you owe us $285." Bucky's trying not to laugh and trying to bring this priest back to earth, so he starts jabbing the guy from behind, yanking on his coat and giving him chops to the spinal cord—all out of camera range. I don't know all that much about Catholicism, but what Bucky was doing had to be *at least* a ve-nial sin. Now the Niagara students are on Bucky's case. "Hey, Coach, let go of the collar!" (A "collar" is Niagara slang for a priest.) Now it becomes a chant, "Let go! Let go! Let go of the collar!"

112

Wait. It gets worse. Now, some wacko in a jockstrap and an Indian headdress and nothing else—apparently a St. John's Redmen fan—goes streaking by Bucky and the priest for his three seconds of fame. That makes the priest do a 180, and while his guard is down, Bucky jerks the mike away from him and throws it back to his play-by-play guy in about .03 second. The reviewers said they had seen more civilized All-Star Wrestling interviews.

But I understand. Trying to do those interviews while the fans are going ballistic and the trumpet section is in your ear isn't easy. One time, Butch van Breda Kolff, who preceded Bucky at NBC, was doing a post-game interview with Providence's star players Marvin Barnes and Ernie DiGregorio. While he was talking to them, some guy reached down from the bleachers and stole his hat. Van Breda Kolff just snapped. He forgot all about the interview, spun around and grabbed the guy and started roughing him up. On camera. Fortunately, he was able to get back into coaching.

Perhaps there is something basically unbalanced about college basketball analysts, because I also worked on NBC with Al McGuire. Unfortunately, Al was a puncher too. He got nervous during stand-ups before the game, and with every point he'd make, he'd punch me in the shoulder. And not just light punches. He'd really slug you. I don't think he knew how hard he was hitting. At times, he was actually terrified out there. He would never, ever, be on camera by himself. I think he punched just to know you were still standing next to him, that he wasn't by himself. Between Bucky and Al, I needed a cut man.

Al McGuire is one of the most wonderful characters in sports. His family ran a grocery store–tavern in Rockaway Beach, Queens, New York. Al was the smiling face behind the bar, keeping everybody laughing and spending. His brother Dick was the great athlete who went on to become a Hall of Famer for the New York Knicks. But Dick was terrifically shy and Al could talk a coyote out of a lamb chop. As things happened, Al ended up becoming even more famous than his brother in sports circles by winning a national championship as the head coach at Marquette in 1977.

Al was a hail-fellow-well-met if there ever was one, but he had his peccadilloes. He could suddenly disappear from places—dinner parties at his house, banquets, whatever—and take long, long walks without telling anyone. He collected toy soldiers. He has one of the great toy-soldier collections in the country. Very serious stuff. He's into re-creating entire battles with 5,000 men and horses and cannons and the works. The only problem was that when we were on the road, he'd persuade *me* to go with him to all these strange people's houses and apartments to buy the soldiers. It was always "We have to stop off just for a second and see about a guy who has the First Battle of Bull Run." And it would always be in some .32 caliber neighborhood where everybody parked on the front lawn. I always thought that's how I'd die. "Two Die in Musket Altercation."

Al was sly. One time, a reporter asked him if he had any superstitions or pre-game rituals. "Yeah," he said. "The first thing I do is count the crowd."

"Is that for good luck?" the reporter asked.

"No," said Al. "It's because I get five percent of the house."

Whenever a salesman would call him at home pitching some product or other, Al would pretend to be very interested and then say, "Hold on just a second." Then he'd put the phone down on the counter and never come back. I've never quite had the nerve to try it, but it sounds *very* satisfying. (Jerry Seinfeld, the comedian, does one that's even better. When the salesman calls, he says, "Yeah, I'm kind of busy right now. Let me have your home phone and I'll call you back." And the salesman always says, "Well, I'd rather not have people calling me at home." Seinfeld says, "Me neither," and hangs up.)

Like a lot of college coaches, Al could tell stories from takeoff to landing. I remember one he'd tell, about Peter Gavett, the coach of the Maine women's basketball team, explaining his team's 115–57 loss to Virginia in his season's opener. "I think the whole game hinged on one call," Gavett said.

Which one, Coach?

"The one I made last April scheduling the game."

And yet Al was like no other college coach I've ever met. He wouldn't watch other college games on television. He wouldn't even watch an NBA game. He did not know many players around the country other than his own. One year, when he coached the Pizza Hut All-Star Classic in Las Vegas, he was hopeless. He didn't even know the names of the stars. He'd just say, "Hey, 14, what's the matter with you? You're a guard, right? Don't give me that stuff underneath."

Al would always tell me, "I don't know basketball. I *feel* basketball." When Michael Jordan was playing for Dean Smith at North Carolina, I personally didn't think he was headed for godlike superstardom. I knew he'd be a star in the league but I never *dreamed* he'd accomplish what he has. But Al always knew. He'd say, "This guy is going to be an enormous star in the NBA." He felt that Smith kept his players in check and that when Jordan eventually got his chance, he was going to break out big. It's the old line. Q: Name the only coach able to hold Michael Jordan under 20 points a game. A: Dean Smith.

I'd hook up with Al when his regular partner, Dick Enberg, had scheduling conflicts. He and Enberg were a terrific team and they had one little secret that's never been told. They were working a game together in Jackson Hole, Wyoming. They were just sitting around together one night and got to talking about why there was no Wyoming State. "There just isn't," says Al.

"Well," said Enberg with a grin. "There is now."

So, with nothing better to do, the two of them created a university. They put it in Kelly, Wyoming (population: 9), named them the Porcupines, made their official colors sky blue and red and even named the place where they play—Coal Arena. It started out as something to while away an evening, but one time Al brought it up on the air. "How about that Wyoming State?" he said. "They've won six in a row up there." Before long, they were getting little press clippings around the country, just little mentions to "watch out for Wyoming State, they're on the rise." One Top 20 poll even had them as a team "also receiving votes."

And then it got crazy. They were working a De Paul–St. John's

115

game and went to a banquet. They planted a friend of Al's at a table and introduced him as the athletic director from Wyoming State. He even had a sky-blue-and-red Porcupine hat. People came up to the guy and said things like "I understand you guys have the inside track on recruiting so-and-so." One man even came up to him and said, "My son went to Wyoming State. He was on the wrestling team there." It was the sporting equivalent of *Being There.* People *wanted* to believe some little tiny school was making it big. They sold shirts and hats and gave the money to charity.

Eventually, it got so big it got scary. There was no way to keep up the charade, so Wyoming State eventually "lost" a few games and fell forever out of the public consciousness, sort of like Mason Reese.

I'm *sure* Bucky and I covered a Wyoming State game in our years together. We covered everything else. My first network broadcast of any sport was in college basketball—Alex English and Mike Dunleavy of South Carolina vs. Manhattan College and its star center, Bill Campion. Still have my chart of that game. Also, the only time my play-by-play was used in a court of law was in college basketball. We were doing a Boston College game and their gunning, rather out-of-control guard was taking some awful shots and I was very critical of him for it. Then one day I get word that my comments on that game were going to be used as evidence in a point-shaving trial. The gunning guard? Ernie Cobb. It was, in fact, the last major point-shaving scandal in college basketball. So they attempted to use my criticism of Cobb's shot selection as evidence that he was dumping the game. I still don't think that was fair. He simply might have been having a bad game. Cobb was then exonerated. In the past, I've questioned various Knicks players' shot selection—like that of former Knick Xavier McDaniel—and nobody thought he was shaving anything but his head.

Broadcasting college basketball was also the only way I've ever almost blown a game. In those days, I would often do a Saturday-afternoon game with Bucky for NBC and then get back to New York to do a Knicks or Rangers game at 7:30. Making the night game was never a problem until the day we did a Holy Cross–Boston College game in Worcester, Massachusetts, home of Holy Cross. We finished the game and jumped back in the rental car and headed to Logan Airport so I could catch the shuttle back to New York in time to do the Knicks game. As we were driving, Bucky said, "You know, Marv, I don't remember the trip taking this long." I insisted it had. We drove on.

Pretty soon, Bucky says, "You know, where do they ski in Boston? All these cars have skis on them." I said perhaps they were having a rally. Just then we saw a green sign that said, "Welcome to New Hampshire." I missed the entire first half and the pregame host Bob Wolff had to sub for me.

College basketball *did* provide me with one of the most dramatic last-second scenarios I had ever witnessed. I'll never forget the Arkansas-Louisville NCAA tournament game of 1981. That was the game in which a reserve player named U. S. Reed of Arkansas made his half-court shot at the final buzzer to knock defending champion Louisville out of the NCAA tournament. Bucky and I called that game. What I remember about it is that the nation almost missed it. The games were regionally split all across the country. But most of the nation was seeing St. Joe's upsetting Brigham Young. As our game kept getting closer and closer to the end, I kept shouting into my headset during breaks, "Better come to us now! Better come to us *right* now!" They barely did get to us before Reed made his impossible shot.

Naturally, they wanted to interview Reed in the middle of the chaos afterwards and Bucky went out to get him. I looked up and Bucky was standing in the middle of the floor ready to do the interview, only he had the *wrong guy*. I started yelling as loud as I could to whoever could hear me, "That's not Reed! That's NOT Reed!" But Bucky couldn't hear me in the din. Finally, I hollered loud enough for one of the floor crew to hear me. He raced off and got Reed and just in time inserted him for whoever it was Bucky had. Two more years of college basketball and I'd be a mime today.

Bucky could be amusing. One time he was talking about the, ahem, unusual sweaters St. John's coach Lou Carnesecca wore.

117

"Louie could do for sweater sales what the Boston Strangler did for door-to-door salesmen," Bucky said. One time we lost our power during a De Paul–Louisville game. When we came back, Bucky said, "Sorry about that, folks. It seems we lost both the audio and the video. In TV, that's bad."

Finally, in 1991, after more than a decade working college basketball Saturday afternoons, NBC acquired the NBA contract and my college days ended. I miss working with Bucky and I miss the atmosphere and the passion of the games. I suppose I will miss everything about college basketball but the pretending; pretending some of the kids are in school for anything but basketball; pretending they want to be in college at all; pretending that basketball isn't their career choice anyway. A reporter once asked Lakers forward Elden Campbell if he had earned his degree from Clemson. "No," said Campbell, "but they gave me one anyway."

It reminds me of the time Texas A&M basketball coach Shelby Metcalf called one of his players into his office. The player had received four F's and a D on his report card.

"Son," said Metcalf, "looks to me like you're spending too much time on one subject."

If you guys can sell this, you can sell anything.

—David Stern

10

Michael Jordan,
Annoyance

The best phone call I ever received in my life was from the president of NBC Sports, Dick Ebersol. "Guess what."

What?

"We got the NBA."

Ever since I was a kid doing games into my trusty reel-to-reel, I've wanted to do network NBA games and that one phone call made it actually happen. I've been around the NBA going on 40 years, when you consider all the time I hung around the playground courts in my hometown of Manhattan Beach, Brooklyn. Almost any day of the week, we could go to those courts and see future NBA legends such as Connie Hawkins and Billy Cunningham play. In fact, the Hawk and Cunningham and I all shared the same blacktop. Of course, they were at Court No. 1 and I never played on anything but No. 3, where the mortals played. But, hey, it *was* the same blacktop. Kids would be lined up five and six deep around that court to watch them and I was usually sardined in there among them. Hawkins was probably the more talented player, but Cunningham had better fundamentals. Hawkins, even as a kid, would stand at the pivot and wheel the ball back and forth over his head, waiting too long to pass it, while his teammates exhausted themselves running circles around him. But in his peak years the Hawk could pull off moves that only the likes of Julius Erving, Michael Jordan and Shawn Kemp have matched.

I've been lucky. I've never been farther than five or six rows back ever since. Basketball is the one sport that lets you get remarkably close. In what other sport do the athletes go flying five rows into the crowd after loose balls? In what other sport can you hear the other players jawing to each other? Larry Bird was *always* jawing. He'd get in a guy's face, make a three-pointer and say something like "I'm just going to drill every one of those tonight. It's over." One afternoon, Charles Barkley was playing and this one black referee was making every call, a few of them against Barkley. When he called another one on him, Barkley walked over to him and said, right in front of us, "Hey, it's Martin Luther King Day. Take the day off. Let the white guys make some calls once in a while."

Actually, there are times when the fans are *too* close. There is an attorney in Washington, Robin Ficker, who sits three rows behind the opponents' bench and drives people crazy. At times he comes with credible information and incorporates it into his arsenal. He never stops screaming at the opposing team's players, coaches, trainers and announcers. He is not a normal person. Pat Riley has wanted to do an anesthetic-free tonsillectomy on him on more than one occasion. When Sam Smith of the Chicago *Tribune* came out with his book *Jordan Rules,* in which Jordan's teammates were sometimes critical of him, Ficker would read passages from it aloud behind the Bulls' team huddles just to see if he could get under Jordan's skin. The guy never gives up. One time Patrick Ewing of the Knicks was killing the Bullets' center, Charles Jones, on his way to a 45-point night. And yet Ficker kept screaming, "Jones is eating you up, Ewing! Eating you up!" What game was Ficker watching? We caught a shot of Ewing on

121

the monitor. He was trying to keep a straight face, but he couldn't.

At least Ficker doesn't swear. In Detroit, Leon the Barber, who died recently, had the mouth of a career sailor. Every other word out of Leon's mouth was unprintable. Leon was so obnoxious that when Hubie Brown coached the Knicks, he used to take the team out into the middle of the floor so his players wouldn't have to listen. (The other reason Hubie did it was so the fans couldn't hear *him* swearing at his players.) When Detroit had weak teams, which was for quite a long time, Leon the Barber would ride *them*. Finally, the Pistons moved their bench across the court just to get away from Leon. Since Leon couldn't move his seat, the problem was solved.

NBA players are almost as talkative. You can ask Barkley about the weather and he'll give you twenty minutes. Former superstar George (Iceman) Gervin was asked how he enjoyed all the X's and O's that came with his new job as assistant coach with the San Antonio Spurs. "Well," said George, "I don't know much about X, but I sure know a lot about O."

Even the coaches are good. Somebody asked Bob Weiss, the one-time Atlanta Hawks coach, how Stacey Augmon was adjusting in his rookie year? "Well, Stacey was a bit disturbed by the salary cap when he came here," Weiss said. "They didn't have one at UNLV."

Darryl Dawkins, the Chocolate Thunder Dunker, could be a very entertaining interview too. Somebody asked him his birth date once and he said, "I'm six-eleven. My birthday covers three days."

He was usually friendly with me during his days with the New Jersey Nets, except once. He was going through one of his periods when the Nets management didn't think he was playing as hard as he should, and, come to think of it, he wasn't playing hard. He was grumpy and didn't want to do the scheduled WNBC-TV interview I had set up with him, but he finally consented. It looked like the end of the line for him as a Net. So I asked him right out, "Darryl, where do you think you'll be a month from now?"

"(Bleep)," he said. "I thought we weren't going to talk about that kind of stuff."

I never let subjects read my questions before the interview, because it ruins the spontaneity of the answers. And I never promise them what we will or won't talk about. So I said, "I never said that."

He walked off. End of interview. Still, it made for some enjoyable home viewing. Luckily, the story has a happy ending. Dawkins stayed with the Nets and took it out on my brother Steve, voice of the Nets, for a long, long time.

Basically, though, NBA players—even the superstars—are willing to talk. In fact, Michael Jordan, at times, comes to find *me* for an interview. Throughout the 1991–92 season, whenever we'd broadcast a Bulls game, we'd get a few players for some sound bites and Jordan was obviously somebody we wanted on. One week, we decided not to interview Jordan. Next thing we knew, he found us in the bowels of the stadium. "Don't you guys want to do an interview today?" Turns out he's superstitious. We'd interviewed him so many times, he'd built it into his routine, and athletes *never* like to mess with their routine. The guy can *really* be a pest.

Jordan is the single greatest basketball player I've ever seen. I'm not sure whether Magic Johnson might win you more titles because of all the things he does for your team, but nobody has ever done more things well than Jordan and that includes Julius Erving, the great ABA and Philadelphia 76ers star. Dr. J did not have nearly the outside game that Jordan has. Remember when Jordan had six three-pointers in the first half in Game 1 during the finals with Portland? Julius was not nearly the defensive player Jordan is. Jordan is probably the greatest offensive and defensive player in the game, something that's *never* been said of anyone else. Not West, not Baylor, not Russell, not Abdul-Jabbar, not Bird, not Chamberlain, not Magic. Julius did amazing things in the air, and so did Elgin Baylor, David Thompson and Connie Hawkins. But Jordan can do anything they did and more.

Johnny Kerr, who now broadcasts the Bulls games, signed Dr. J out of the University of Massachusetts when Kerr was the general manager of the Virginia Squires of the ABA. Kerr says there's no comparison. "Michael is a vicious offensive player," Kerr says. "Doc was never a vicious player. He was a finesse player." Kerr played, coached, managed and broadcast. "I've seen all [Jordan's] games in the league," he says, "and he still does things that bring me out of my seat."

Jordan is so great that you can tell there are nights when he plays mind games with himself to get motivated. Larry Bird used to do that too. Bird would say to himself, "Tonight, I'm going for nothing but assists." It was a challenge he'd issue to himself. And he'd run off 19 assists and only score 11 points. Other nights he'd say, "Tonight, I'm going to be a three-point shooter and run off five in the first half." Jordan does that now. He plays a game within a game. Some nights, he'll be the scorer, some nights the defender, some nights the playmaker, some nights a three-point shooter. Like Wayne Gretzky in hockey, he reinvents the game. Gretzky made an entire offense out of setting up behind the goal. One night, against St. Louis, Gretzky was hemmed in on both sides by defensemen. They weren't coming after him, but they weren't letting him out from behind the net either. Stuck, Gretzky did an amazing thing. He flipped the puck over the top of the net and off the unknowing backside of St. Louis goalie Mike Liut and in for a goal. Jordan has done that with his incredible changing of hands on the way up and his spectacular dunks. He's even reinvented the free-throw rebound. Sometimes, maybe once every three nights, when his own teammate is shooting, Jordan will set up at the top of the circle, as usual. Only this time, as the second free throw is on the way, he'll come flying up next to him, step into the lane a fraction of a second after he shoots, sky toward the rim and, if he gets the right bounce, jam the rebound home. All perfectly legal and absolutely riveting.

Remarkable people sometimes try to remain unremarkable people off the field just to keep some sanity in their lives. NBC's Ahmad Rashad is one of Jordan's best friends and he says Jordan's friends now are the exact same friends he had in high school—Michael's brother Larry and a few others. He appears as loyal to them now as ever. When the Bulls won their first title in

1991, he bought them all championship rings. During the NBA finals with Portland in 1992, Jordan had them all out for the games. One night, after Game 3, according to Ahmad, Jordan and Larry played *serious* one-on-one at Nike headquarters in Beaverton, Oregon, just outside Portland. Here was Jordan, the greatest basketball player on earth, banging against his brother in the middle of the finals. That was the same finals in which his friends staged a game and even hired a cameraman to record the action. It was Jordan.

Michael Jordan is probably not like you think he is. He eats like a parakeet ("I starve hanging out with him," says Ahmad) and sleeps like an owl, maybe five hours a night. He lives in a very normal house in a very normal neighborhood outside Chicago. It has no gates in front, no pool, a two-car garage. There are weights in the game room. Against all odds, success really hasn't perceptibly changed him.

What has changed about him, though, is his basketball game. He came out of college without much of an outside shot. He developed a very good one. He was getting roughed up by teams such as Detroit, and consequently, Chicago was consistently losing to Detroit. So he decided to make himself stronger. He became a fanatic about weight lifting. In fact, during the Olympics in Barcelona, he lifted so hard that he got too tight and it affected his shooting.

Now Jordan and the Bulls routinely beat Detroit, which must prove satisfying, especially since there has always been friction between him and Pistons stars Isiah Thomas and Bill Laimbeer. Everybody knows the rumor that Thomas convinced his All-Star teammates to freeze out Jordan in his rookie-year All-Star game. As for Laimbeer, he ripped into Jordan after Jordan told NBC's Quinn Buckner that he felt like Chicago was "America's Team." "Who cares what he says?" Laimbeer said. Well, nobody except most of the basketball-watching world.

I don't know if it was that or something else, but Laimbeer will rarely do pre-game interviews with us now. Apparently, he feels that TV has made him out to be a bad guy and the Pistons as a fighting, overly aggressive team. "That's wrong," he said. "Why can't you accentuate the positive?" And yet Laimbeer himself has used his thug image as a marketing tool. Laimbeer came out with a violent video action game, which was backed by television commercials showing violent basketball action. I mean, I wouldn't want to hurt *sales*.

Laimbeer and I have crossed swords before. In 1991, the Pistons were supposed to play a Christmas Day game at Chicago, but because several Pistons didn't want to give up their Christmas Eve, the team voted to charter a plane and arrive the day of the game. Naturally, we reported it on the air. It's fine to want to stay home on Christmas Eve, but anytime you travel the day of the game, you're going to be a little more drained than normal. That's a given. Laimbeer was upset we mentioned it on the broadcast. Sorry, but it could have—might have—affected the game.

I have a similar sort of disagreement with Portland Trail Blazer fans. The Blazers are loaded with talent, but each year they seem to make too many mistakes in the playoffs and lose. In 1990, they lost to Detroit in the finals, four games to one. In 1991, there is no question they should have beaten an Abdul-Jabbar-less Lakers team in the Western Conference finals—even the Lakers' Magic Johnson said so—and didn't. In 1992, they lost in six in the finals against Chicago. In an interview I did during that regular season, Bulls coach Phil Jackson basically said that whenever you get Portland into a close game, they "self-destruct." I guess our crew didn't help matters by putting a reverberator on the word "self-destruct." Jackson later regretted saying it, but I don't think he regretted thinking it.

That's about when the "racism" overtones crept in. On the *Arsenio Hall Show* one night, the Blazers' best player, Clyde Drexler, said that anyone who says the Blazers are a "dumb" team is racist. I like Drexler, but that's hogwash. I talked with a lot of black players in the league who thought the same thing, including Magic. Is Magic racist? The Blazers *do* make bad decisions down the stretch, primarily because they don't have a true point guard running the show. Terry Porter is a shooter, a scorer, but not a true point guard. Playmaker Rod Strickland has the

126

same kind of profile as the whole team: great talent, bad decision maker. Is this a guy you want running your team, a guy who has a history of being late for practices, buses and team flights? When then–San Antonio Spurs coach Larry Brown traded for Strickland from the New York Knicks, I asked him if he was worried about Strickland's penchant for tardiness. "Nah," said Brown. "The good thing about San Antonio is, you're only ten minutes from the airport wherever you are." Ten minutes must not have been enough. One season later, he was in Portland.

The other reason Chicago has dominated recently is their coach, Phil Jackson. I never thought Phil Jackson would become a coach in the NBA. I say that because I was with him for 10 seasons with the Knicks and I always figured him for head of the Montana Fish and Game Department or perhaps a correspondent for *The Village Voice*. I always thought he was antsy to get on with a different life once he left the NBA. He was one of the most curious guys I ever knew. He'd always ask questions. He constantly asked Holzman about defense. He'd listen to my play-by-play calls of the Rangers games and then have fifteen questions about hockey for me the next day. When he missed the entire 1969–70 championship season, he became friends with Garden photographer George Kalinsky and learned all about photography. Every game that year, you'd look over at the bench and not be able to find him. Then you'd look along the baseline with all the photographers and there he was, shooting pictures. I half expect to see him some nights on the baseline at Bulls games, reloading.

He was a voracious reader. On the road, he was like Bill Bradley. He was a walking Barnes & Noble. And if he wasn't reading, you'd find him across the concourse discussing the meaning of life with four guys in turbans. Later, when he became the Bulls coach, he presented every player with a list of books they should read before the season was out. It went over about as big as it would have on any other NBA team—like a lead balloon.

But I think his ability to be a good listener helped him win his three titles. He surrounded himself with excellent assistant coaches—Johnny Bach and Tex Winter. Winter, former head

127

coach of the Houston Rockets, designed the offense. Bach helped design the defense, which is one of the most finely orchestrated in the league.

It's Lesson No. 1 you learn in the NBA—talent only takes you so far. Wilt Chamberlain had far more talent than Bill Russell, but I still rank Russell as the better center. Russell had limited offensive skills, but he did more to help his team win than Chamberlain ever did. Chamberlain's numbers were staggering—50.4 points a game in 1961–62—but then he'd hurt you with his foul shooting. Or he'd take his fall-away jumper. Knicks general manager Eddie Donovan loved it when Chamberlain took that fall-away jumper because, when it missed, his back-pedaling follow-through took him all the way *off* the court, leaving him in no position to get a rebound and allowing the opponent to sometimes set up an easy fast break.

Off the court, though, I liked Chamberlain far more than Russell. Chamberlain did have a wry sense of humor. Not long ago, there was a wild rumor that the Knicks were considering signing Chamberlain even at his advanced age. Somebody asked Wilt about it. He thought about it and he finally said, "How would Ewing adjust to being the backup?"

As a Knick ball boy, I can remember how rude Bill Russell was with the fans. He had this thing about not signing autographs, which was all right, I suppose, but it was the *way* he turned kids down. He was very gruff about it, not even looking at the kids. He always said it was a philosophical decision, that kids shouldn't want autographs of sports stars, they should want autographs of their teachers and parents and policemen. But, just recently, Russell announced that he was going to finally begin signing autographs—for a $2 million contract with a sports memorabilia company. Apparently, teachers just aren't that important anymore.

To me, Russell is the antithesis of a guy like Magic Johnson, who always has time for everybody, fans, reporters, friends, whatever. It's amazing, though. The last guy I thought I'd be sharing a microphone with for the 1991–92 season was Magic

Johnson and yet, when he retired from the NBA with the virus that causes AIDS, he was suddenly wearing an NBC blazer.

Most athletes who are just out of the game and in front of the mike are afraid to be objective, but Magic isn't afraid to criticize players. From the very first game he broadcast, he was outspoken. It was a Lakers game and he criticized former teammates Byron Scott for his shot selection and Elden Campbell for not asserting himself enough offensively and not working hard enough in practice. At first, Campbell's public reaction was annoyance. But then we got word that suddenly, quietly, Campbell was putting in extra time at practice. After all, this *was* Magic talking.

I have never discussed Magic's HIV condition with him, but I remember one night when it affected his performance. We were doing a game in Portland and he just wasn't himself. His mind wasn't into it. He wasn't as sharp as usual. Then we found out his wife, Cookie, was about to have their baby and the doctors wouldn't know until the baby was born whether it too would be HIV-positive. No wonder he was so distracted. He took a charter flight back to L.A. after the game and Cookie delivered the next day. The baby was fine. When he rejoined us, Mike Fratello and I came to rehearsal sucking on pacifiers. Also, just to make Magic feel at home, "the Czar" cried intermittently throughout the telecast.

Anyway, the point is, doing network NBA games has been all I'd hoped it would be hanging around the No. 1 court at Manhattan Beach, aching to be a part of it all. Actually, it's been better. It's been easily one of the greatest thrills of my life. So to pay Dick Ebersol back for choosing me, I saved his life.

We were in Paris for the McDonald's Open, a pre-season exhibition tournament that featured Magic and the Lakers. I was on the same plane with Dick and his wife, *Kate & Allie* star Susan Saint James. It was rainy when we landed in Paris. As we were riding to the hotel on one of those high-speed superhighways, our limousine started making sputtering sounds. We suggested that perhaps we pull over. The driver didn't so much as turn his head. After another minute, the car died right in the center lane of the highway. Cars were whipping by us at 110 kilometers an hour and we're sitting there like road kill waiting to happen. We all smelled gas fumes. Still, nobody seemed the slight bit alarmed at these lovely developments. In fact, Susan took out a book to start reading. Here we are, our lives are in very real and immediate danger and Susan decides to catch up on her light reading.

Personally, I felt very much like panicking. I started saying, "We should get out of here!" Nobody seemed to be listening. I started *yelling*, "We should get out of here!" Nothing. I screamed at the driver, "We've got to get out of this car!" I finally convinced them that we could die in this car in the middle of the highway, so, finally, the first chance we got, we made a mad dash for the shoulder. The driver refused to come with us. Not thirty seconds after we'd reached the grass on the side of the road, we heard a huge crash. A car speeding on the highway didn't see the limo and smashed into it. The limo was totaled.

Dick ran back near the car and was sure the driver was dead. He wasn't. We later found out he had merely passed out. The ambulance drivers took him to a hospital. He had suffered serious injuries but would end up fine. It even made the *National Enquirer*. Yes, it did. "Sportscaster Saves Lives of TV Exec and Star!" It was right there, next to the story headlined "Chicago Mom Gives Birth to 7-lb. Eyeball!"

A *very* proud moment.

In all of show business, there is one thing that bugs me more than any other: I have performed on the Letterman show more than any other comedian. And yet Marv has been on seven or eight more times than I have.

Now, my appearances take me 100 hours to think up, not to mention flying 3,000 miles to the East Coast to do the show. I mean, don't get me wrong, I love doing it. The Letterman show gave me an audience. But when I go on, I do four minutes of stand-up, which is not easy.

Now Marv gets called, generally, when the guy from the Columbus Zoo has to go to a peacock's funeral or he calls in sick or something. So they call upstairs. "Marv, can you do nothing but get one of your *slaves* to put together a jokey tape of ballplayers hurting themselves, or maybe throwing a bat and beheading someone, and come down and do the show tonight?" And Marv says yes, and pushes a button and gets a slave into his office and says, "I'm doing Letterman in two hours. Get my shot ready." And in two hours, he's doing it.

This, in comparison to what I do, is such a joke to me. And I think you can now see why I have had to triple my therapy.

—RICHARD LEWIS

11

The Emergency Backup Guest

Of the over two dozen fans I have on the face of the planet, at least half are among the four-and-under set. This is both because of my (a) longtime work with the diminutive Mike (the Czar of the TeleStrator) Fratello on the NBA on NBC and (b) my command performances on the well-respected drama series *Sesame Street*.

Of course, when the Children's Television Workshop people came to me originally, they talked in terms of a romantic lead. But I felt it wouldn't be proper for the image. Instead we settled on play-by-play of Gladys the Cow jumping over the moon. I still believe it's some of my best work to date.

Since then I've done quite a number of appearances on *Sesame Street,* including my now classic "jalopy" appearance. Gordon, an actual human, Oscar the Grouch and Grundgetta, Oscar's girlfriend, are trying to go to a Knicks game. But misfortune strikes. Oscar's broken-down jalopy collapses halfway there. The car stays broken and, unfortunately, they can't even listen to the game because the radio is jammed. They're stuck. Luckily, I happen to see them on my way home from the game and ask if they need any help. Gordon recognizes me right away.

"Don't you know who this is?" Gordon says to Oscar.

"No," says Oscar, gruffly.

"This is Marv Albert! That's his voice you hear doing the Knicks games!"

"Who cares?" Oscar grumbles.

I end up giving them a ride home and discussing the highlights of the game with Gordon. I got along well with all the actors, except Oscar. I felt a certain tension there. Things got a little testy. There was a shoving incident. We nearly came to blows.

The difficult thing about working *Sesame Street* is that there's a man and a woman lying on the floor operating the puppets and you have to keep eye contact with the puppets and not the operators or it ruins the scene. Still, I believe working with puppets helped in the work I did with "the Czar" on NBA broadcasts.

Besides, the great thing about doing these shows is that they repeat them over and over. For instance, after I taped the first episode, I was amazed how many times my brothers Steve and Al told me they saw it.

I'm very big with pre-literates. I appeared regularly in animated form on the Saturday morning cartoon flop known as *Pro Stars*. I was the ubiquitous announcer who was always around when the three heroes, Wayne Gretzky, Michael Jordan and Bo Jackson suddenly become engaged in some competition or other. Fratello, a very big Saturday-morning-cartoon fan, pestered me every day until I agreed to ask them for a bit part for him. Then, when they agreed to it, he *insisted* they draw his character nearly as tall as mine. What a prima donna. We appeared in the same scene together and had to do the voice-overs at a sound stage. In cartoons, everything has to be wildly exaggerated, so Mike and I were absolutely *screaming* at each other when we taped our segments. Personally, I enjoyed every second of it.

I believe I've also made literally tens of fans through my work with the *Late Night with David Letterman* show. I am proud to say I have made more appearances on Letterman than any other single guest, owing to one single talent: I was right down the hall during his NBC days. I have appeared with a month's notice and with three hours' notice. I am a designated bailout for them. In fact, one time they were doing a "viewer mail" segment. A viewer wrote in wanting to know what happens when a guest doesn't show up. Letterman said, "Oh. Follow me." He got up from his desk, walked down the hall, made a right turn and came to a giant glass case. On the glass it read: "In case of emergency, break glass." Letterman took the ax and broke the glass. Out stepped me.

Dave likes to use a few people—Tony Randall, Connie Chung, Tom Brokaw, me, Regis Philbin—as his "Letterman Players," if you will, faces he can throw in every now and then as little surprises. One time, they did this bit in which Letterman was hit by a drop of water from above. The ceiling was leaking. So Dave decided to go to the floor above and check it out. The cameras followed as he went up a staircase, walked down a hall, opened the door and found me in there, asleep, with a cigar in my mouth, immersed in a bubble bath. They even had peach bath towels hanging from the racks with the letters "M.A." monogrammed on them. Letterman woke me up. "Marv, what are you doing?" Whereupon, I groggily explained that I was watching highlights of the World Football League matchup between the Montreal Machine and the Birmingham Fire and must have dozed off. Motivationally speaking, it was not an easy scene for me to do, especially since Letterman insisted that my being nude in the bath was "essential" to the script.

I've been appearing on Letterman since January 2, 1984, when I came out and pointed out the superiority of pro wrestling. "Dave, these guys can *really* take a punch." Since then I have appeared so many times, it feels like home. I have been introduced on that show as everything up to and including the former WBC light heavyweight champion of the world. One night, they had me do this bit making fun of how many times I'd been on. Dave was interviewing another guest and they had me walk on the set, unannounced, apologize quickly, ask the guest to get up from the chair, fish out my wallet that I'd left in the chair there from the night before, apologize quickly again and leave. A man needs his wallet.

What's zany about Dave is that he will laugh at anything I say. He's the absolute easiest audience in the world. But he's a worrier. Sometimes he goes out onstage just before the show to say a couple words to the audience, just to see what kind of crowd it's going to be. And when the audience is bad, I've seen him get down right away. He'll just drop. He'll come back and say, "This is going to be a rough night." He's usually right, but he has the uncanny ability to pull it out.

Of course, there are a few drawbacks in doing the Letterman show and one has been the intrusion of the comedian Richard Lewis into my life. Richard is the former co-star of the TV series *Anything But Love* with Jamie Lee Curtis and is second only to me in Letterman appearances. He is absolutely, hands down, the world-record holder for leaving long messages on your answering machine. And his messages are just like his act. Beep. "Marv, my life is in shambles . . ." and off we go. Usually, it's something horribly serious, like he can't get his VCR to stop flashing "12:00."

Richard is a devoted Knicks fan. The problem is the Knicks thing. He asks for tickets to specific dates on next year's schedule when next year's schedule isn't even done yet. He'll call up and say, "The Bullets are in town two years from Wednesday. Can you get me some tickets?"

He once asked his therapist, "Is my relationship with Marv worth it or will it take years off my life?"

"Did he get you four tickets?" the therapist asked.

"Yes."

"Can he get me some?"

The man is so insecure. He lives and dies by the number of NBA stars who acknowledge his existence on any given night. One time, after a spectacular basket, Kareem Abdul-Jabbar pointed to Richard in the first row as he ran down the court. Richard was beside himself until Kareem began pointing at every single person in the Garden that night. Richard blamed that disappointment for his, as he says, "tremendously poor sexual performance" that night.

Richard belittles the Albert Achievement Awards I do on Letterman as opposed to his three-minute comedy bit, but bloopers are an unrecognized art form. I wasn't the first to do bloopers, but I was one of the first, and as such, I think I have the right to say that blooper shows have really gotten out of hand. On one blooper show, I saw a race car crashing, flipping over and over, augmented by dubbed-in screeching tires and crashing glass. That's not funny. That's sick. The rule I and my crack staff, headed by Dave Katz, have adopted is: no auto accidents and no athletes getting injured. We do allow, however, an occasional boxer getting slugged below the belt. That falls under our Rule 16B: "protective-cup exclusion."

I first became appreciative of the humor of a groin shot at 13 years old in a street hockey game in Brooklyn. I was playing goalie. It was the final seconds of the "championship" game. We were ahead 4–3 and one of the stars of the league came in on a breakaway and took a low, hard slap shot. It hit me right in the groin. I didn't know anything about protection back then. Everyone went wild but I went down. I never felt so much pain. Thus the common hockey phrase: Groin save and a beauty!

Let's see Richard Lewis do a bloopers show. Dave Katz spends *days* sifting through videotape for just *one* Albert Achievement Award highlight, not to mention the four hours it takes him to edit it. The guy has seen so many mountains of tape that if he laughs at a clip, you know it's very, very funny. You show him the one where the gymnast Brian Meeker slips and plows straight into the vault. No laugh. You show him the one where the minor league outfielder runs *through* the fence. Nothing. The hockey fight in Calgary where the two guys square off for thirty seconds and never fight. Zippo. Tom Watson swinging and missing? Nope. The guy losing his pants going for a foul ball? Zilch.

Next to the possibility of grown men losing their pants, Letterman seems to find unbalanced amusement in my trademark phrase "Yesssss!" I'm afraid "Yesssss!" has leaked out from the world of sports. I don't know how many times Macaulay Culkin said it in the movie *Home Alone* but I know I'm still waiting for the royalty checks. It has replaced "All right!" in the American idiom. It is part of the language now. *You mean your mother-in-law is moving out? Yesssss!*

Letterman is infatuated with "Yesssss!" One night, his writers came up with this bit where he would punch a little red button on his desk that, when punched, would roll a tape of me delivering an enthusiastic "Yesssss!" Of course, he got a little out of hand with it. He hit it once. "Yesssss!" the tape of me said. He hit it twice. "Yesssss!" it said twice. He hit it three times. Four times. Finally, I rushed angrily out onstage and snatched the button away. "Do you mind?" I snapped. "I'm *trying* to do the sports!" But the truth is, I love it when he hits that little red button, because I get a residual check in the mail about two weeks later. He'll be talking to Kathy Ireland. She'll say something. He'll hit the button. I get a check. Jerry Seinfeld. Button. Check. It's a wonderful arrangement.

The first "Yesssss!" I ever uttered was at the end of the third quarter of a Knicks game in 1968. Dick Barnett hit a long bank shot at the buzzer and I said, "Yesssss!" People started repeating it back to me the next day, and the next thing you know, it was part of my repertoire. I got it from the onetime colorful NBA ref Sid Borgia. Whenever a player would get fouled while shooting, Sid would stick up his hand and holler, "If it goes . . . Yesssss!" In other words, "If it goes in the basket, I'm going to give this guy a bonus free throw! . . . Yesssss!" Poor Sid. I don't believe he ever received any royalty checks either.

I do not go around handing out "Yesssss!"es indiscriminately. The shot must warrant it. A lay-up or a free throw is not a "Yesssss!" But a 24-foot jumper in a close game is. Any strange, off-balance or impossible shot is. Cazzie Russell of the Knicks used to have this line-drive style of shot that seemed to work perfectly with the "Yesssss!" In fact, I think he got more "Yesssss!"es than any other player in the NBA. To this day, his stationery has his name and the word "Yesssss!" written next to it.

People seem to love to say it. Every now and then, somebody

will come up and want do an impression of me and, unfortunately, cannot be dissuaded from letting me hear it. I have been standing at the urinal in a men's room and had the guy next to me start doing an impression. What am I supposed to do, clap?

Whenever someone does one, I simply give them a rating between 1 and 10. The best ever was Billy Crystal—an 8. Very strong. Bob Costas is an 8 too. Roy Firestone is a strong 7. Most people are about 4s or 5s. And they all do the 1969 Knicks. "Frazier across the time line, cross-court to Bradley, underneath to DeBusschere, the running one-hander . . . Yesssss!"

A few years back, the Knicks even conducted a sound-alike contest. Hundreds of people sent tapes. They chose my color partner at the time, Butch Beard, as one of the judges. Butch said that his cat refused to be around when he'd listen to the tapes. The cat would disappear for long periods of time. After the contest, they found him in the basement. They were not sure he was going to live.

One time, according to my ex-wife, Benita, the family was listening to the tapes in the kitchen and listening to my call of that night's Rangers game on the radio at the same time. One of the kids—I'm still trying to find out who—mistakenly thought my live performance was one of the sound-alike tapes and said, "Man, throw that guy out. He's *awful.*"

My personal favorite was a man named Mike Mackin, a Kearny, New Jersey, warehouse foreman, whose rendition was me rushing out of a Schaefer beer commercial to call a bang-bang Rangers goal. "That's Schaefer, the one beer to have when you're having more than one OFF-THE-FACE-OFF-THE-RANGERS WIN-THE-DRAW-AND-SCORRRRRRE!"

Billy Crystal's accountant had me saying, "Larry Brown on hand tonight. Rumor has it he's changed his seat location four times." Wow, Billy Crystal's accountant sure can write funny stuff, don't you think?

The contest winner was the public relations director at Roosevelt Raceway, Barry Lefkowitz. He did an impression that was ridiculously good. Maybe that's why Roosevelt Raceway is out of business now. His grand prize was getting to do half of a quarter of play-by-play in my place. And in just those eight or so minutes he learned what I have known for years: John Andariese is a *very* annoying person.

In America today, it is amazing what they will let a sportscaster do. For instance, I interviewed President Bush in the Oval Office. This was for an NBC baseball pre-game show. Did you know Bush started at first base all three years at Yale? He was good field, no hit. Did you know he played against Vin Scully? Did you know he once got a hit off Milt Pappas (in a celebrity game)? Did you also know he threw out the first pitch at a Houston Astros game and it bounced halfway to the plate? "Hey," he said sheepishly, "it broke a little early." He was awfully cordial. He even took my family on a tour of the White House.

The next day when my son Brian explained to his ninth-grade teacher where he'd been, she wouldn't believe him (wink, wink). So she sent the President a school absence form to fill out. Bush sent it back properly filled out and also wrote a note on the bottom: "No makeup. Brian learned a lot here."

Another for instance: They let me play for the Washington Generals against the Harlem Globetrotters once. The Globetrotters were a huge thrill for me when I was a kid. In fact, I remember the devastating disappointment I felt when, working as a Knicks ball boy, I happened upon the Globetrotters practicing some tricks with their archrivals, the Generals, hours before the show. Talk about disillusionment.

Playing in my one game for the Generals, Generals coach Red Klotz kept insisting how serious they were about winning. Right. *What are we, 1–2000? Just a little slump.* During the game, Meadowlark Lemon of the Globetrotters kept yelling at me, "Get the *hell* out of our reams!" I guess I had happened into the middle of one of their comedy bits. He was not happy with me. I also remember having a wide-open jumper from the corner for what were sure to be the only professional hoops points of my life. But just as I shot, a 'Trotter named Bobby Hunter flew out of nowhere and rejected it. I hope Bobby Hunter is happy. I live daily with the shame.

They even let me on *Hollywood Squares*. Somewhere between

I'd Love to But I Have a Game

Joan Rivers and Zsa Zsa Gabor was me. It was very easy to do. Every American should be on *Hollywood Squares* once. I've done little comedy bits here and there on *Saturday Night Live*. I still think I could come on as a musical guest. A little "Malagueña" might go over big then.

Then there was my motion-picture career that started and ended with *The Fish That Saved Pittsburgh*. It was so dreadful, it disintegrated on video shelves all over this land. Gene Shalit saves a clip of one of my scenes as one of his all-time ten worst ever. I'll spare you the details, but it was basically about a basketball franchise known as the Fish. It starred Julius Erving, Stockard Channing, Debbie Allen, Flip Wilson, Jonathan Winters and Harry Shearer, who went on to much bigger things with The Simpsons. Harry was my broadcast partner (Murray Sports). All I can say is, I was horribly miscast. I played myself.

There is, however, one thing I am extremely proud of, and would like now to take a serious moment to discuss: my sandwich at the Stage Deli in Manhattan. It's a triple-decker of corned beef, Swiss cheese, cole slaw and Russian dressing. You scoff, but at the Stage you work your way up the menu. The longer you're on the menu, the higher you go. You fall out of fame, your sandwich is history and everybody behind you moves up one notch. I have been hanging around so long that I am No. 1, which tells you a lot about either the sorry state of fame in this country or the disturbed people who run the Stage Deli.

Still, even with my own sandwich, I am occasionally subject to humiliation. One night, the gorgeous sex symbol Morgan Fairchild was supposed to introduce me at a middleweight fight in Atlantic City. She got on the mike and said, "And now, here's Merv Albert."

We're *very* close.

For coaches, broadcasting is basically Purgatory. It's just some place we have to go until somebody will give us a real job. I admit it. I've had to go to that place myself. I worked as a color analyst with Chick Hearn on the Los Angeles Lakers broadcasts for two years. You may remember my unforgettable line I often repeated in those years: "That's right, Chick." I even worked a year on the NBA on NBC. And it's funny, but every now and then, I get to wondering what it would be like to be a sportscaster full-time, to make an actual career out of it. I visualize myself doing it every day, as Marv has done. And when I do, I think to myself: "You gotta be kidding me."

—PAT RILEY

12

This Book Brought to You by . . .

Whatever goes wrong, when anything goes wrong, there is one rule in sports that usually never fails: Blame it on the media.

Now, the media is often wrong, but not nearly as wrong as most athletes think. One time, former heavyweight champion Mike Tyson got an angry look on his face upon being introduced to Dave Raffo, the boxing writer for UPI. "One of your trucks ran over my dog," Tyson yelled at Raffo. Tyson looked like he might take a swipe at Raffo, but one of Tyson's aides quickly said, "No, no, Mike. That was UPS."

Professional athletes must deal with the media almost every day, yet a lot of them really don't understand how we work. Thurman Thomas, the All-Pro running back for the Buffalo Bills, is famous for dodging interviews. Doesn't matter who you represent—newspaper, radio, NBC—he'll dodge you. Whenever we'd ask to speak to him a day or two before an NBC telecast as part of our preparation, he'd always have some excuse not to do it.

He'd never say no, he just wouldn't ever do it. Which is fine. Nobody has to talk if they don't want to talk. But then Thomas would turn around and complain that he doesn't receive the deserved national publicity. He feels it has cost him MVP awards. Can't have it both ways.

Actually, Hot Rod Hundley, the slightly skewed Utah Jazz announcer, *did* have it both ways once. He was supposed to do a post-game interview that would be heard by the several hundred loyal fans hanging around the arena after the game. Darrell Griffith was scheduled to come out and do it, but Griffith stiffed him. So Hundley decided to play both parts. He'd ask a question, move over to the other chair, pretend he was Griffith, answer the question and move back again. By the end, the fans were giving him a standing ovation *and* he kept the post-game gift.

It always amazes me the number of guys who, during their careers, don't seem to take the time to talk to the media and then, as soon as their careers are over, want to *become* the media. Kareem Abdul-Jabbar, as great a player as he was, never was overly friendly with the media. He's a very bright guy, but for most of his career he never let anybody know it. His attitude was usually arrogant. That was fine. But as soon as he had a book out, he was Mr. Congenial. Then, following his retirement, he wanted a job in broadcasting. In fact, Terry O'Neil, executive producer of NBC Sports, interviewed him for a job. Here's a guy who wouldn't say two words about a stirring game he'd just played and now, suddenly, he figures he has what it takes to be a color man. Who knows, he might just end up being good. Bill Laimbeer can be arrogant and combative too, and I think he'd make a superb color analyst. He would be extremely entertaining.

There are some broadcasters in the business who wouldn't touch a negative story with a forty-foot pole. For a while my color man for New York Knicks broadcasts was the former Knicks general manager Eddie Donovan. He shied away from any negative commentary. For instance, I might say, "A small crowd on hand tonight." And Eddie would quickly add, "But not *too* small." If the entire court suddenly cracked open in the mid-

143

dle and swallowed all the players, Eddie would've called it a "minor plumbing problem."

Eddie had a vested interest in the club. But some broadcasters won't do it because either they're apprehensive about getting on the wrong side of the clubs they cover or, in fact, the station they work for pays for rights for the broadcasts and the guy doesn't want to jeopardize the contract. That makes it doubly tough on those who believe in being objective, because the athletes get used to puffball questions from guys afraid to rock the boat. When a tough question comes along, some athletes lash back.

But I think New York is different, especially working at Madison Square Garden. Bob Gutkowski, president of the Garden, has always been very strong about objectivity. He believes that you can't fool the New York fan. If a team isn't playing hard or a guy is dogging it, you better say it, because a lot of the fans already know it. The late Sonny Werblin, flamboyant former president of the Garden, would kid me about my style. One time, during the 1970s, when the Knicks were pretty weak, he came up to me and said, "I really enjoy your announcing. But do you *have* to be so damn objective?"

Rick Pitino, currently the coach at the University of Kentucky, wrote in his book that when he was head coach of the Knicks he would turn the sound down on the videotapes of their games so the players couldn't hear the comments my color partner John Andariese and I made. He didn't want anything negative to reach their ears. He wanted the announcers to be fans, as he pointed out, in the manner Johnny Most was during all those years with the Boston Celtics. Did he want me to lie when the team wasn't playing well? Was it always that the other team was playing so well and had it nothing to do with the Knicks playing poorly? Give me a break. You can't b.s. the fans. It's a bit ironic too, because Mike Fratello was on Pitino's staff then and complained occasionally about our "negativism" on the air. But when Mike joined NBC to broadcast NBA games he picked up a different understanding of the business and became one of the more objective analysts.

Gutkowski always insulated me from team executives who

would become upset over on-air remarks. Al Bianchi, the Knicks general manager for a time, was particularly bothered by some of the opinions expressed, but he'd complain to Gutkowski and Gutkowski wouldn't pass it on. He felt that the broadcasters should have an independent philosophy.

There were those in the Knicks organization, for instance, who thought my willingness to report what I knew hurt the team's chances to acquire Kareem Abdul-Jabbar from the Milwaukee Bucks in 1975. I found out and reported that the Knicks were very close to getting him. The Knicks, in fact, thought they had the deal wrapped up and that's what I said. Well, apparently, Milwaukee didn't like the Knicks' "arrogance"—a frequent complaint about the Knicks front office in those days—and killed the deal. In the end, Abdul-Jabbar went to Los Angeles. And the Lakers went on to win five titles.

Once, on NBC, we were doing a game at Boston Garden, one of the best places on earth to broadcast—the acoustics are good, the crowd is into it, the building has character. But one bit of "character" about the place that is not so wonderful is that the floor is about as level as Lombard Street in San Francisco. There are all kinds of crazy hops on the floor, crevices that shouldn't be there, bumps and humps a visiting player has no idea to watch out for. It's actually a bit of an unfair advantage for the Celtics. To prove it, we had a cameraman put his camera on the floor and use a measuring device to show how uneven the floor was. Some of the floor crew for the Garden were upset that we were doing it. In fact, during the game, there was some sabotage done to our power cords, causing us to go off the air briefly. I'm not saying it was them, but that was awfully coincidental.

Still, I'm sure we'd do it again. To me, the most important asset a sportscaster has is his credibility. Once you've blown it with a listener, it's very hard to get it back. Harry Caray, who broadcasts the Chicago Cubs, is from the old school. He's a character in himself, an entertainer. He figures that's the agreement you enter into when you flip him on. One time, a ground ball bounced off a Cub pitcher's head and right to the waiting shortstop, who turned an easy double play. "Cubs win!" Harry

145

shouted. "The good Lord wanted the Cubs to win!" The Lord must have been having a *very* slow day.

Of course, sometimes it doesn't matter how objective you are. People will think you're biased. We heard that frequently during the Chicago Bulls–Portland Trail Blazers finals of 1992. Fans from both sides were *convinced* we were secretly biased for the other team. One viewer wrote to *The Sporting News* complaining that I was rooting for the Bulls. I sent a letter back. "Dear Editor: I've always enjoyed your fine publication, but next time Mike Fratello writes you, I wish he'd sign his own name."

Walt Frazier, now the color analyst for the Knicks radio broadcasts, understands credibility. In 1992, the Knicks had just beaten Detroit in the first round of the playoffs. Play-by-play man Jim Karvellas went very upbeat with his tone at the end, *very* enthusiastic, and Frazier said to him, "Why are you celebrating? They haven't done anything yet." They got into an on-air argument about exactly how momentous the win was. I'm not sure either of them was right, but at least it was an issue. In some towns, *both* guys would have been pouring the champagne.

The other thing that bothers me in announcing today is commercialism. It's not as blatant now as it was in the days when announcers were constantly throwing in commercial plugs, even letting it intrude in their play-by-play. In those days, sportscasters pushed products *during* the action. Whenever someone hit a home run in a Mel Allen game, it was a "Ballantine [beer] blast." Red Barber had his "good as gold, good as an Old Gold [cigarettes]." Russ Hodges had his "He hits into Chesterfield [also cigarettes]." And Marty Glickman had his "good like Nedick's." Nedick's was a chain of hot-dog-and-soft-drink stands. "Good like Nedick's" became so popular that public-address announcers began using it for free.

Nowadays, commercialism still sneaks into broadcasts. On NBC football broadcasts, for a while we had "Budweiser kickoffs." As in "This kickoff brought to you by Budweiser." Not only was it tacky (exactly who was kicking off, the Clydesdales?); it was hypocritical. Here was the NFL, whose rules won't let an active player advertise an alcoholic beverage, letting a beer own every kickoff. I felt so foolish saying "the Budweiser kickoff" that I once said, on the air, "The word 'the' is also brought to you by Budweiser." To their credit, NBC and Budweiser eventually came up with another vehicle. The Budweiser kickoff was eliminated.

We still have to do, however, the "Tonight on NBC" promos. I'll do them, but I stage my own little underground war. For instance, I'll scratch out their adjectives, especially if one of them is the word "great." Seems like every Sunday-night show is "great." I don't say "great" unless something is truly "great." "Great" is greatly overused. To me, it better be truly "great." I'll go an entire week of games without saying "great." And I guarantee you, I'm not going to use one up on the next *Adventures of Mark and Brian*.

The networks have to be especially careful about how intrusive they move into a fan's enjoyment of a Sunday-afternoon game. We're already accused of making NFL games excruciatingly long with all the commercials. I once had a Saturday night off and sat in the stands to watch a Giants-Jets exhibition game. It was a local game, not network, but I had no idea how many television time-outs a crowd has to endure. It's funny, but it feels just the opposite in the booth. The NFL is so paranoid now about the length of the game that if you have a 90-second commercial spot, at 92 seconds, bang, they're out of the huddle. That makes it very difficult to do anything except play-by-play. You'd like to do more dressing up of the broadcast with short interviews and vignettes. "It was a stormy week for Marcus Allen, who lashed out at Al Davis . . ." And then go to a sound bite of Allen. But there's rarely time for that these days.

The instant replay rule died by the same sword, which is too bad, because I liked the idea itself. The problem was that, practically, it was undoable. First of all, it took too long. Second of all, it came attached with too many ethical thorns. For instance, smaller-market games—say Seattle vs. Indianapolis—were broadcast with fewer cameras. That meant replay officials sometimes had as few as four camera angles to choose from on the replay, as opposed to, say, the Giants vs. the Raiders, which might get

147

ten. Does the fact that you play in a big city mean that you corner the market on justice?

Another for instance: Network producers and directors controlled which pictures were shown to the replay booths. There was always the remote possibility that a director or a producer could be wagering on the game. If he bet on the Bills to cover the spread by 10 points and this Jets touchdown would make the spread only 9, is he going to show the angle that proves it's a touchdown? For that matter, what about a producer who can sense that if this touchdown is allowed, he has a blowout on his hands and he'll start hearing TV sets clicking off all over the country? Would he show the angle that winds up hurting the ratings?

There was another problem. The NFL told us that the replay officials would not listen to the audio of the telecast so as not to be influenced by the commentators. However, I *know* they did listen to the commentators. One of my analyst partners, Bob Griese, knew the rules cold and was very well-respected by football people. Whenever he'd comment on a pending instant-replay decision, he'd always be perfectly objective and straight. And he was usually right. The replay officials were trying to make the right decision too, so they'd listen to what he said, for our telecast was piped into their booth. After the game, they'd discuss it with him. "You were right about that," they'd say to Griese. "That was a good point you made."

At least the NFL had some sort of policy about instant replay. Other sports seem to operate on a "let's make it up as we go" system. In boxing, we'll go to locations where they'll suddenly decide to use instant replay to solve a ruling dilemma. During one fight, the referee was unsure how to rule on a penalty point, so he came to us at the table and said, "I'm just going to look at the replay and decide." I had to say, "Wait a second. You can't just suddenly decide to *invent* a replay rule." I've seen it happen in college basketball too, where the officials will come over and check the replay to see if a player got the final shot off before time had expired. True, videotape is probably a hundred times more accurate in deciding that than a human being, but if that's the case, then allow for that in the rules. Personally, in the NBA, I think if you said you could look at the replay in that situation and that situation only—not for foul calls or traveling or anything else—it would be a good idea.

The point is that the networks get accused of intruding on the game—changing the game itself—when, occasionally, it really isn't the networks' fault. For instance, in the L.A. Lakers–Chicago Bulls finals a few years back, the power for our feed went out in the second quarter. In effect, we were off the air throughout the country. The arena was fine. The lights were all working and so was the scoreboard. But the referee, Darrell Garretson, decided he would hold up the game until our power came back. Here were 20,000-some people and two teams twiddling their thumbs waiting for our cameras to start working again. It's exactly what the media critics complain about: the cameras *changing* the very event they're trying to capture. It's like a protester sitting on the sidewalk until the cameras arrive and then jumping up and throwing rocks through windows. We couldn't talk to our truck and we had no line to New York, so we were stuck. After a few minutes, I roped Fratello into telling Garretson that this wasn't right, that we had to let the game go on. And so the game went on. After a few minutes our power returned and we picked up the game in progress.

Fratello likes to tell that story—the day he waved his wand and restarted the NBA finals. I now occasionally call him "the Commish."

I suppose I am lucky to be working with "the Commish," or anybody else, for that matter. When I first began doing network broadcasts, I don't think the country was ready for my voice. It's a different type of sound. In my earlier years, I recall, one TV critic wrote that it sounded like a piece of chalk scraping across a blackboard. That was quite a confidence builder. Actually, as things turned out, I think my voice has been more of a plus than a detriment because it's so different. I don't sound like just about anybody else you hear in any part of the country. You wouldn't believe how many people actually *like* the sound of chalk scraping across a blackboard.

I'd Love to But I Have a Game

Since I didn't have a perfectly modulated presentation, I had to rely on my voice explosion and my ability to describe the action fast and furiously. Marty Glickman gave me a wonderful tip once and I still live by it on radio today: You should be able to close your eyes and describe the court to your listeners. For instance, "He goes across the midcourt line, dribbling right to left in front of us." There are points on the court, like places on a map, and you mention them each time the ball passes through—the lane, the key, the time line, whatever. You're everything to the listener. There are baseball announcers who drive me crazy. Anytime a guy strikes out, they say, "Strike three!" But you don't know if it was a called strike or a swinging strike. *Now* tell me I don't have a life.

I don't want to do a Sermon on the Mount thing, but the problem with a lot of play-by-play guys today is that many of them just jump straight to television without ever doing radio, so they don't have that *feel* for the game. Nor do they have the ability to speak quickly and describe what somebody is doing. TV does it all for them. But when something is happening the cameras can't see, or the video goes out, they're scrambling and the listener suffers.

The basic play-by-play for television is more sparse. There is less a feeling that you *are* the game as there is in radio. In TV, you merely have to be succinct and set up your color man. You're pretty much just identifying the player with the ball. But you can still do it with distinction. Ray Scott used to do that best in the championship era of the Green Bay Packers. He had a spare, simple elegance that still held tingles. "Starr . . . Dowler . . . Touchdown!" What separates television play-by-play people is their ability to give you little qualitative judgments. "Good shot there. Not a smart shot there." And to give you the background information that might suddenly be relevant. "Dickerson is having words with his linemen. He publicly criticized them two weeks ago." I'd say I only use a tenth of the notes I have prepared for any game. I knew an announcer who used to come in with reams of notes. And each time he would mention one of the notes, he would take his pen and check it off. His color man must have loved him.

As long as I'm complaining, there is one last thing I'd like to get off my chest. Stats. Guys overdo stats. Stats are overrated. You can pretty much do anything with stats you want to. As Woody Hayes used to say, a fellow could very easily drown in a river whose average depth was only three feet.

One time, Bob Uecker, when he was catching for the Cardinals, went on Harry Caray's post-game show. Uecker had hit a ball off the shortstop's glove and the official scorer had ruled it an error. "I guess you would have liked to see them call that one a hit, eh, Bob?" Caray asked.

"Well, I always like to count 'em as a hit myself," Uecker explained. "I count everything—hits, walks, fielder's choices, everything. If I hit the ball good, I count it."

"Well," asked Caray, "by your own system, what are you hitting right now?"

"Six forty-three," said Uecker.

What do I know about Marv? I worked with him for four years. I mean we never had dinner together or anything.

The guy is always in some fabulous suite with a grand piano, a basket of fruit, and fourteen couches. And what's he doing in there? Writing up his four millionth roster chart on the Indianapolis Colts vs. the Green Bay Packers.

The man has no life. I suppose we could go out to dinner some night, but what am I gonna talk to him about? I don't do a lot of jump balls. Leave me out of it.

—PAUL MAGUIRE

13

A Few Fries Short of a Happy Meal

I have broadcast football for NBC for 14 years now, several of them with Paul Maguire as my partner. Paul is a very disturbed person. He is to sophistication what the *Exxon Valdez* was to shrimp. He likes to swear, drink, chew tobacco and burp. And that's just in the booth. Paul once barked at the police dogs at Rich Stadium in Buffalo. On the air, Paul would get peeved at somebody in the truck and scream into his headset, "Don't make me come down there and get you!" One time, coming out of a commercial just before a Kansas City Chiefs game, I threw it to Paul on the field. He was standing there holding a microphone and wearing an elaborate Indian headdress. I decided to play it totally straight. Never mentioned a thing about the outfit. All I said was "Paul, what do you see as the key matchups for today's game?" And he gave them to me as if nothing in the world was abnormal.

Once, Paul was ranting and raving about something that made

no sense at all, I had to stop him. "Paul," I said slowly. "You've lost control. And it's *early*."

He was a wide receiver at The Citadel, where he led the country in receiving touchdowns in 1959. Of course, this was just after the birth of the forward pass. He was also a punter and a linebacker with the San Diego Chargers and the Buffalo Bills. He is one of only nineteen players who played in the AFL from beginning to end. He started four years for San Diego and yet, one year, made only $8,000. "Christ," Paul would say, "I've seen Jim Kelly tip that much." After one of those championship seasons, he went to Sid Gillman, the notoriously parsimonious coach of the Chargers, to ask for a $1,500 raise. Gillman told him to take a seat. He turned off the lights and ran three minutes of 16-millimeter film showing every single dumb and/or rotten play Paul made the entire year. He did not get the raise. In fact, "by the time I walked out of there," Paul said, "I felt so low, I wanted to give *him* money." NBC executives now use the same trick.

Gillman used to be obsessive about film. He once told Bum Phillips that watching game films was better than making love. To which Bum replied, "Either I don't know how to watch films or you don't know how to make love."

San Diego was such a drawing card in the old AFL that in one game in Los Angeles Paul's first year, a throbbing crowd of nearly 4,000 came to the Coliseum to witness. That left only about 100,000 seats empty. So pathetic was the attendance that ABC, televising the game, moved all the fans to one side of the field to keep it from looking so paltry. Whenever the ball was in the air, ABC took the cameras off it for fear of showing the acres and acres of empty seats.

As a punter, Paul wasn't bad. One time, in the Houston Astrodome, Paul averaged 45 yards on 11 punts. "I think I did my best punting in the second and fourth quarters," Paul said, "when the air conditioning was at my back.

Paul also holds one NFL record you can look up: most bottles of beer drunk, career. It happened in San Diego. A bunch of his Charger teammates were in a bar called Bully's on La Jolla Boulevard. Just as they were leaving, a bunch of guys from the New England Patriots walked through the door: Babe Parilli, Gino Cappalletti, etc. In those days, there were only a handful of teams, so everybody knew everybody. Paul and his motley crew turned around and walked right back into history. For that night —the only night anybody in restaurant history can remember it happening—the whole lot of them drank up *every bottle of beer* in the house. It'll all be in the movie version of Paul's life.

I blame most of Paul's emotional problems on Dick Butkus, the great Chicago Bears linebacker. Butkus is the man who once said, "I wouldn't ever set out to hurt anybody deliberately unless it was, you know, *important,* like a league game or something." Or, for that matter, an exhibition, which is what Chicago and Buffalo were playing on this day. Paul was a punter. Butkus liked to rush the punter. Paul went back to punt and got it off safely. Watching the punt, he didn't see that Butkus had peeled noiselessly behind him. When Paul turned to start filling his lane, Butkus hit him a crushing blow that could be heard in Columbus. Paul was laid out flat on the ground but his shoes were still in the turf. The neurologists feel certain that some crucial synapses in his brain were snapped. As Paul lay in a prone position, trying to decide if the 12-yard line at Cleveland Stadium would be a good place to be buried, Butkus told him, "You've got to pay attention."

This, I believe, goes a long way toward explaining the way Paul behaved during our wildly popular "Paul Relates to the Players" segments on NBC pre-game shows. Since Paul was a former player, we decided to let him get inside the players' heads, to show what the game is like inside the pits. One of the first "Paul Relates to the Players" was a segment with the Washington Redskins' huge lineman Joe Jacoby. Paul asked Jacoby if he would demonstrate some of the holding techniques that are prevalent in the NFL. Jacoby agreed, took hold of Paul's NBC blazer and said, "This is the jersey hold," and jerked at it. The entire coat ripped down the front. Paul stared in disbelief.

Another week, at Soldier Field in Chicago, there was some serious question about the condition of the field. It was very muddy and nobody was quite certain what cleats would work, so we asked Paul to investigate. Adorned in jacket and tie, Paul decided he should try to run a little on it. Unfortunately, he tripped and went flying face first into the mud. Sadly, he appeared to enjoy it.

Finally, Paul did some serious relating to Keith Willis, a behemoth lineman of the Pittsburgh Steelers. Paul asked Willis to demonstrate some of the illegal moves that go on in the pits. Paul even wore a helmet for this one. The problem was, the helmet was too small for Paul's rather *oversized* cranium, so Paul took the pads out, leaving three protruding screws on each side. Willis was ready. He started with the finger-in-the-ear-hole trick, then the head butt. These looked like they hurt Paul plenty, but Willis hadn't yet gotten to the head slap. Paul didn't think Willis would really slap him, but Willis really did slap him. Very hard. It was a devastating blow, in fact, right up the side of the head. Paul looked like a man in an earthquake. His legs were rubber, his eyes glazed over, spittle dotted his chin. What with those three screws on each side of his head, it must have turned his skull into a colander. Naturally, we laughed riotously, but Paul came up from the ground with teeth clenched, faced purpled, fist balled. We got the impression he was rather upset. Eventually, cooler heads prevailed. About then is when I told Paul, "Uh, we weren't sure we got that on tape. Could you do it again?"

I believe that was the last installment of "Paul Relates to the Players."

If some of the color men in the league are a few french fries short of a Happy Meal, so are a lot of other creatures that populate pro football. It is, after all, a very strange game with very peculiar habits. Warren Moon, quarterback of the Houston Oilers, once revealed to us that whenever the Oilers change centers, he requires a lot of time during training camp getting used to taking snaps from him. "I know it sounds weird," Moon explained. "But everybody's crotch is not the same. You have to find that niche."

You did not get this kind of great stuff in *The Boz*.

Then there was Richard Dent. After the 1985 season, I presented Dent, defensive lineman of the Chicago Bears, the keys to a brand-new car from *Sport* magazine in recognition of his Most Valuable Player award in their Super Bowl victory over the New England Patriots. Dent accepted the gift gratefully, stepped to the podium and said, "I just want to thank *The Sporting News* for this brand-new car." Other than that, it went perfectly.

One time, ABC's Ara Parseghian was doing an Alabama game and said of the Tide's new coach, "It's not easy replacing a living legend." Bear Bryant, of course, had been dead for two years. The opposite of that is what former analyst Harvey Martin, the former Dallas Cowboy, said during a Buffalo Bills–St. Louis Cardinals telecast. Martin said that Bills running back Booker Moore had "recovered from a fatal disease." Apparently so!

If analysts can be a little out of touch, they're nothing compared to some NFL coaches we run into. Some of these guys tend to let entire decades slip by unnoticed. Former Washington Redskins coach Joe Gibbs, for instance. Great coach. Nice man. But obsessed. When Gibbs went to his first training camp as the Redskins head coach, he took his eight-year-old boy with him. Unfortunately, once Gibbs got immersed in the camp, which was right away, he completely forgot about the boy. After three days, he happened to see his boy in the cafeteria, his clothes filthy, his face covered in chocolate, running around like a boy raised by wolves. He'd just completely forgotten he'd brought him. To this day, I'm not sure he knows where that child slept for those three days.

Gibbs, like a lot of NFL coaches, believed he could get an edge if he could just stay a little later and look at one more film than the other guy. He used to sleep three nights a week at his office, but he might as well have made it seven, since even on the nights he went home, he didn't get there until 11 and even then he started watching more film as soon as he got there. A few years ago, his wife decided to make cassette tapes of their dinner conversations so her husband could have *some* idea of what was going on around the house. But one night about a week into it, his wife began telling him something, and the more she spoke about it, the madder she got, until, finally, she was yelling at him on the tape. Thus, another family-togetherness idea was scratched.

Gibbs admitted once to having no idea who Oliver North was. Later, somebody asked him if he'd ever heard of Madonna. "No," he said. "It's not like Oliver North, is it?" A reporter asked him casually how his relative's recent wedding was. "I won't know until I see the films," he said. Is it any wonder burnout got him?

Ray Perkins, the ex-Tampa Bay coach, was in the Gibbs mode. One time, a friend asked him if his wife objected to his 18-hour workdays. "I don't know," Perkins said. "I don't see her that much." Dick Vermeil, former head coach of the Philadelphia Eagles and a current ABC-TV football analyst, was like that, obsessive. They tell the story that late one night Vermeil was watching films as usual with a few assistant coaches. When a routine out-of-bounds play trundled by on the tape, Vermeil jumped out of his chair and yelped, "Wait! Roll that back a little! O.K. . . . Now forward a little . . . Right there! Freeze it!" He went to the screen and pointed to a teenage boy standing on the Eagles sideline. It was his own son. "Boy, has *he* grown," marveled Vermeil.

Of all the football voices at ABC, there was none quite like Howard Cosell, my first contact in broadcasting.

Cosell was abrasive even then. When I was doing the weekly radio show with him, he'd call the night before the show and say, "Are you *sure* you're going to be there?"

"Yes, sir, Mr. Cosell, I'll be there."

"No. That is not good enough. You must be *sure*. Are you absolutely *sure* you're going to be there?"

For some reason, he has been a very bitter man and never seemed to enjoy his success. He was always as rude and unpleasant as he could be to people, especially everyday kind of people—elevator operators and receptionists and network technicians. Years later, when I was just starting out in the business, I called him up and mentioned that I had been a regular on his kids' radio show. "I wonder if I could ask you some advice about my career," I said.

158

I'll never forget the heartwarming word Howard Cosell passed on to me that day.

"I don't care about you," he said. "I get calls like this all the time. Guys like you are a dime a dozen." Then he hung up.

Cosell had his day. He changed sportscasting for good with his opinions and candor. I suppose he changed it for the better. But apparently he wanted all sports broadcasting to cease the day he quit.

Actually, when you consider the first televised football game I ever did, I am lucky *my* career didn't cease a long time ago. It was in the old Continental Football League, which went the way of Nehru jackets and the Edsel not long after. It was the Brooklyn Dodgers (the Brooklyn *football* Dodgers) vs. the Philadelphia Something-or-others at a soccer field on Randalls Island. I truly believe Kermit the Frog could have done a more professional job than I did that day. Not to make excuses, but here are a few excuses: For one thing, I was so far from the field, I couldn't read the numbers or, for that matter, the yard-line markers. It was a night game and it was so dark that on handoffs you really couldn't see who had the ball. *Reportedly, this is Smith on the sweep.* I'd pray for pass plays in the hopes of actually glimpsing the ball. However, I thought I excelled at punt returns. For another, I hadn't heard of more than one or two players. Most of them were just a collection of guys trying to make the NFL, which, come to think of it, was what I was trying to do. I misidentified people, got the score wrong, couldn't find the ball and just basically set football broadcasting back about 15 years. This is true: I thought my career was over.

It wasn't until the mid-1970s that I tried football again as the radio voice of the New York Giants on WNEW. I worked them for four years, including their last two games at Yankee Stadium and the (cough, cough) thrilling games at Yale during their forgettable years waiting for Giants Stadium to be built.

My color man on the Giants telecasts was Sam Huff, the legendary Giants linebacker and Hall of Fame inductee. Huff was something of a curiosity in the NFL since he was no bigger than your average cornerback nowadays. But he was a remarkable player. For some reason, it seemed like he could stop Jim Brown any and every time he came his way. There was this ragged notion that Huff got credit for a lot of tackles he only came late to, but it was unfounded and it never seemed to bother him. In fact, he joked about it. He used to like to tell the story on himself about the time Giants teammate Erich Barnes tackled Eagles running back Timmy Brown. Brown kept hollering at Barnes, "Get off me! Get off me!"

"I can't," said Barnes. "Not until Huff gets here."

The other terrific guy I met through the Giants was the punter Dave Jennings, who now does color commentary for the Jets. Jennings loves to tell stories, especially the one about the day in 1980 when Giants coach Ray Perkins sat them all down for a speech. They'd just lost five in a row and things were looking bleak. Perkins said, "Fellas, this summer, I happened to see a fighter named Yaqui Lopez. He fought this guy for fourteen rounds and he got the daylights beat out of him in every round. I mean, he was bleeding, his eyes were swollen shut, everything. But Yaqui Lopez *would not* quit!" Perkins was beginning to get worked up as he spoke. "In the fifteenth round, he answered the bell and he could hardly walk, could hardly stand up! And yet he came after the guy and stayed after him! And you know what? *He knocked the guy out!* I gained so much respect for him that day that I decided that's what I want my team to be like—to keep fighting and doing whatever it takes until you give yourself a chance to win." By now, Perkins is General George S. Patton himself. "Gentlemen, Yaqui Lopez is fighting again today on television after practice. I want you guys to watch him!" Well, Perkins had the players so jacked up that the minute practice was over they all went flying into the players' lounge and flipped on the fight. Here he was, Yaqui Lopez, their inspiration, ready to fight. And there he went, Yaqui Lopez, knocked out in the first round. Some guys hadn't even found a place to sit yet and the whole thing was over. Their faces fell flatter than tortillas. The next day, the Giants went out and played in the great tradition of their inspiration: They got creamed by San Diego, 44–7. Said Jennings afterwards, "They shoulda stopped it."

William Hurt hung around for a few weeks to learn the TV ropes before the filming of *Broadcast News*. © *Madison Square Garden*

Utah Jazz coach Frank Layden broke into our Knicks-Jazz pre-game show to "examine" my ailing throat. On the right is my MSG network color partner John Andariese, who put him up to it. Neither of them are well. © 1990 R. Allen Schnoor/Sportclik.

In Monaco just before the Barcelona Olympics with Larry Bird, Prince Albert of Monaco and Patrick Ewing. Larry and Patrick are smirking because they've just given the Prince a Hot Foot.
© Andrew D. Bernstein

Mike Fratello, the Czar of the Telestrator, has become an American Icon. He's starting his own Summer Fantasy Telestrator camps— where they serve one hot lunch per day. © *National Broadcasting Company, Inc.*

At my 25th Anniversary Night at the Garden. Left to right: that's me, my father Max, son Brian, daughters Jackie and Denise, son Kenny, Marty Glickman, Referee Sid "Yes!" Borgia and my former color partner, Butch Beard. © *George Kalinsky*

A rare photo of my NBC football partner, Paul Maguire, without his parole officer. He eventually learned to eat with a knife and fork.
© *National Broadcasting Company, Inc.*

Ahmad Rashad diligently prepares for another NBC Broadcast.
Courtesy of Marv Albert

David Letterman discovers the source of the leak above his desk.
Because Letterman insisted I be nude, I demanded a closed set.
© *National Broadcasting Company, Inc./Ray Bonar*

Jerry Seinfeld—obviously not aware of the Garden's dress code.
© *George Kalinsky*

A lanky left-hander from Yale lets NBC pre-game show producer Les Dennis and I try to make out the signature on his old first-baseman's glove. We decided it was Marv Throneberry. © *National Broadcasting Company, Inc.*

Then there was the Giants' famous plane flight back from Seattle. One third of the way home, the Giants' charter started having problems with the landing gear. The captain came on and said there was some question whether they could get the landing gear down. He said they wouldn't know for sure until they got down to 1,000 feet. "In the meantime," the captain said, "we want you to prepare for an emergency crash landing." Upon hearing that, one of the married players began tearing apart his little black book and throwing it into one of the trash receptacles in the galley. Whatever happened, I guess, he didn't want anybody to find it, especially his wife. Just as he was done ripping it up, bit by bit, the captain came back on. "Good news," he said. "We're at a thousand feet and there's no problem. The landing gear is down and locked."

Not two seconds later, the married guy was seen digging desperately through that trash bin, trying to put the little tiny pieces back together.

Unfortunately, three of his teammates were there to beat him to it.

All of which reminds me of one of the all-time football-player stories around. One night, Alex Hawkins, the longtime NFL character, went out drinking and carrying on and doing stuff he probably shouldn't have been doing. When he stumbled in about 6 A.M., his wife was there waiting for him.

"Where the *hell* have you been?" she growled.

"Well, you won't believe it," Hawkins said calmly. "I got home about one, a little tipsy, so I just laid down in the hammock on the front porch for a second. I just now woke up and decided to come in."

"I took that hammock down two weeks ago," snarled his wife.

Hawkins thought about that for a moment and then said, "That's my story and I'm stickin' to it."

I just *love* working with Marv.

I *love* how his right leg gyrates madly under the table while we're on the air, spilling coffee all over my crocodile loafers.

I *love* how he relished getting national network laughs at my expense.

I *love* how he takes up the entire table with his notes and leaves me none. And even *that* is not enough, so he files anecdotes in his pants pockets.

If there is a God, some say Marv will come to a crucial point in a big game, reach quickly into his pocket for one of those anecdotes and blurt out, "Inspected by number twelve."

—MIKE FRATELLO

14

The Dreaded List Chapter

Guessing conservatively, I'd say I've spent an average of 175 days a year away from home. Over 27 seasons, that works out to over six years of my life on the road. I had some scientists at Columbia University calculate it and they estimated that I had gone through a Greyhound-busful of pillow mints. And so, if you never listen to another thing I say, you would do well to get out a notepad and Bic pen and take down my . . .

TEN COMMANDMENTS OF TRAVEL

1. Always get the aisle.
2. If the hotel you're staying at doesn't have (a) bedside lamps you can turn off without pulling a rotator cuff to reach, (b) a phone in the bathroom and (c) 24-hour room service, pack your things and leave immediately.

3. Always leave the bathroom light on. This is also known in various parts of the country as the Les Dennis Rule. Les Dennis produced NBC's baseball pre-game shows and, reportedly, always slept in the nude. In the middle of the night once, he got up and staggered toward the bathroom, totally discombobulated. He had not left a light on. He opened a door, stumbled through it and let it close behind him. He began to wake up a little more when he realized he was in the hotel hallway. Locked out. Naked. With nothing to cover him up but a "Do Not Disturb" sign. Les slunk down the hall until he found the maid's closet and covered himself with a sheet. We all thought it was funny, until Les pulled the same stunt in the next two dozen towns. No, no, no.

4. Never wise off to the skycaps. Paul Maguire, reacting to a slightly rude skycap, did this once. "Did you go to college for this job?" Paul asked him. Paul is still trying to negotiate with a man in Abu Dhabi to get his suitcase back.

5. If there is any trouble with the plane, no matter how slight, the largest man on the aircraft will panic the most. Especially if he is an athlete. Any tiny thing goes wrong on an airplane and athletes are clawing at the emergency exits. There is a famous story about a flight carrying the old Kansas City Chiefs. It looked for a while like the plane was going to have to make an emergency landing. Huge, 280-pound men were blubbering like infants. The pilot announced that the runway would be covered with foam as a precaution. Hearing that, Bobby Bell, the great linebacker, leaped up from his seat and screamed, "I'm allergic to foam!"

6. If you order the beef, the chicken will be better. If you order the chicken, the beef will be better. I'm not sure why airline food has to be so bad. I believe it's an FAA regulation. As such, we try to live by the philosophy: "Airplane food can be fun." So, on a flight between Chicago and Portland for the 1992 NBA finals, someone, mysteriously, ordered "the Czar" a special Hindu meal. Everybody was getting their steaks or their chicken and they brought Mike what looked like part of a hermetically sealed de-

ceased camel. Mike said later he thought if he put his fork in it, the oxygen mask would drop down. I wonder who that was?

7. If you land early, your gate won't be ready.

8. The person next to you may have a warm smile, look extremely interesting and be incredibly well dressed. I don't care. *Do not say anything to him.* You will only get a three-hour discussion about his gout. Usually, I have to get my player-information charts done. One time, on a four-hour flight, I was making up the Denver Broncos' chart. The man next to me, bless him, hadn't said a word the entire flight. Finally, just as we were about to land, he leaned over, pointed to the name of Denver's left guard and said, "Not worth a damn."

9. Ninety-nine times out of a hundred, the in-flight movie will be terrible. The one time it's good, the pilot will come on with some lame announcement just when Alec Guinness is about to explain how he knew which psychotic twin killed the Girl Scout leader.

10. If your cabbie has stopped talking, he's lost.

If it weren't for the road, I'd never get my mail read, and I do receive some bizarre mail. I get people who want me to send them my doodles. I get people who want me to write my own obituary and send it to them so they can put it in a book of "autobiographical obituaries." *Marv Albert, age unknown, died Thursday from reading one too many stupid letters.* I get very bad movie scripts in the mail. The most recent was somebody from Disney—*Disney!*—that wanted me to do play-by-play of two people having sex. I don't care if it was Dean Jones and Suzanne Pleshette, I'm not doing play-by-foreplay.

The best one I ever got, though, was this one in the mid-eighties:

Dear Marv,

I'm in trouble and I'm sitting in the office at my school. The principal is making me write you a letter while I sit here. I would like to know if you could send me an autographed picture that I could put up on the school bulletin board with the other pictures that other students in trouble had to write for.

Sincerely yours,
Scott Cady

Dear Scott,

I'm enclosing an autographed photo. I just know from now on you'll be a good boy because you don't want to go through the turmoil of writing away for another autographed picture. In fact, if your behavior doesn't improve, your principal may have to take the final step—the most severe punishment of all —writing to request an autographed photo of "the Fight Doctor," NBC's boxing analyst, Ferdie Pacheco.

Best of luck and stay away from the school office.
Sincerely,
Marv Albert

I used to collect autographs myself. I'd send postcards to athletes asking for signatures. Remarkably, most of them responded. Comedian Billy Crystal told me he was an autograph freak as a kid too. He said he had Mickey Mantle, Wilt Chamberlain and three Guy Sparrows (a onetime New York Knick that only fanatics and Guy's family would recall). One time, at a Yankee game, he asked the famed announcer Mel Allen if he'd sign his program. "Not now," said Allen. "I gotta wash my shirt." I gotta wash my shirt? So later on Crystal became a star and the producers from Allen's weekly syndicated program, *This Week in Baseball,* wanted to borrow Crystal's "You look marvelous" song. Crystal told them, "Only if Mel Allen gives me the autograph he denied me in 1957." Allen sent him a ball that said, "You look marvelous, Mel Allen. How 'bout that?"

Lee Trevino, the golfer, was in a bar once and a woman kept telling him what a great golfer he was, best in the world, unparalleled. Would he sign something for her? Trevino said sure, what do you want signed? The woman had nothing for him to write on, so she took a five-dollar bill out of her purse and said, "Lee, if you sign this, I will treasure it always. I'll hang it in my bedroom and look at it every night before I go to bed." So Trevino signed it. Twenty minutes later, he was buying a beer and got it back in change.

The whole sports collection thing has got out of hand. Not long ago, a St. Louis disc jockey was auctioning off the tip of former St. Louis Blues player Paul Cavallini's finger. It was sliced off by a slap shot from Doug Wilson of the Chicago Black Hawks. Apparently somebody stole it out of the pathology department at the hospital where Cavallini went after the accident. Perhaps I'm a neophyte at this, but exactly how much do finger remnants fetch on the open market?

Most autographs just get tossed in a drawer or crumpled up anyway. What people should want from celebrities is more of an *experience*. Like, every now and then on the road, somebody will come up to me and ask me what events I remember the best, treasure the most. I never have a very thorough answer, but I've been thinking about it and now, at absolutely no cost to you, I've decided to compile my . . .

5 GREATEST EVENTS I EVER WORKED
(Presented, for drama, in reverse order)

5. Boston Red Sox first baseman Bill Buckner letting a routine ground ball roll through his legs with two outs in the bottom of the ninth inning in Game 6 of the 1986 World Series. An out there would have won the championship for the Sox. Instead, the New York Mets won and went on to win in Game 7.

4. Los Angeles Dodger Kirk Gibson's dramatic home run in Game 1 of the 1988 World Series to stun the Oakland A's and rocket them off to a 4–1 Series triumph. Gibson had been hurt and hadn't played all night. In fact, we at NBC figured the game was over. Bob Costas was already in what appeared to be the losing Dodgers' dugout and I was standing next to the apparent hero of the game, Oakland's Jose Canseco, ready to interview him. That's when the Dodgers sent Gibson hobbling out in the bottom of the ninth to pinch-hit with two outs. And I remember,

when Gibson hit it, Canseco said, quite simply and elegantly, "Oh, shit."

3. The Chicago Bulls' Michael Jordan's three-point explosion in Game 1 of the 1992 NBA finals against Portland. Easily one of the greatest single performances I've ever seen. Ironically, I'd seen him lighting it up hours before in warm-ups and so I asked him in a pre-game interview if he might consider trying some threes that night. "It's possible I might look into that," he said. He looked into it. As he made his sixth straight, he winked directly at Mike and me and held his palms up in a shrug, as if to say, "What can I do?"

2. Tie: The stirring Game 5 of the Knicks' 1970 NBA finals playoffs with the Los Angeles Lakers . . . and . . . Game 7 of the same series, in which Willis Reed limped on the court against all odds and Walt Frazier came up with the greatest game of his life.

1. The Sugar Ray Leonard–Thomas Hearns title fight of 1981 in Las Vegas. I hosted the closed-circuit telecast and witnessed one of the most remarkable come-from-behind performances in boxing history by Leonard. Both fighters tried to fight the other's style, with thrilling results. I remember Leonard's corner man, Angelo Dundee, revving up his fighter in the hot late-afternoon Las Vegas sun. "You're blowing it, kid! You're blowing it!" In the end, he wouldn't.

When you travel as ridiculously much as I do, you have a lot of time to make up lists. You fantasize. You daydream. You ache for a place to set your weary bones down. In this way, I have been able to waste thousands of valuable hours and come up with . . .

THE 20 THINGS THAT MAKE A PERFECT HOTEL

1. Quiet lobby. 2. Quick elevator. 3. Great pillows, large and fluffy. 4. Fresh sheets. 5. Two separate lines on the phone. 6. Voice mail. 7. Good soap. 8. Way too many towels. 9. ESPN. 10. CNN (May I just take this moment to address hotel manag-

ers of the nation: *Headline News is not CNN!)* **11.** TNT—for NBA telecasts. **12.** Blackout curtains. **13.** Great coffee shop. **14.** Freshly ground Colombian coffee served outrageously hot. **15.** Fresh orange juice. **16.** Remote control. **17.** Celery tonic. **18.** A nice tuna on rye. **19.** Twelve different newspapers available. **20.** Checkout cashier who thinks your bill is being taken care of by the American Orthodontic Association convention.

Unfortunately, no hotel has all that. The Westwood Marquis in L.A. comes close, as does the Four Seasons in San Francisco and the Ritz-Carltons Marina del Rey and Laguna Beach. Caesars Palace in Las Vegas has a coffee shop I would roller-skate naked through four floors of Macy's to get to. But until they figure out a way to melt all those hotels together, nobody will have it perfect. Therefore, I have come up with a very sophisticated and analytical way to rank hotel chains. I call it my . . .

SOPHISTICATED AND ANALYTICAL RANKING OF HOTEL CHAINS

1. Ritz-Carlton: Really, really good.
2. Four Seasons: Very good.
3. tie, Westin and Hyatt: Pretty darn good.
4. Marriott: Good.
5. Sheraton: No good, too old.
100. Ramada: Awful. Forget it. Change your plans. Change your career if you must. Just *do not* stay at a Ramada.

I may not be able to join people for dinner (I'd love to but I have a game), but I still have to *eat* dinner. Usually, it's standing at some counter in some stadium wolfing down a hot dog next to a man flossing his teeth with his business card. And so it is that, unfortunately, I can offer you, for this chapter and this chapter only . . .

THE 5 BEST HOT DOGS IN SPORTS
(Not Counting Deion Sanders)

1. Tiger Stadium, Detroit. Absolutely the best. They know how to get them good and charred, the way I like them. If the Tiger stadium hot-dog stand would allow it, I'd set up a cot in the back.

2. Montreal Forum. For big games, they rise to the occasion.

3. Boston Garden. Very good. A lot of it, I admit, is the ambience of the place. It's real New England, with the old building as backdrop and the vendor always getting a little gruff with you. I like to be insulted a little when I get my hot dog. I'm from New York.

4. Milwaukee County Stadium. This is Costas's favorite. He likes the bratwurst. Says it's the best in the country. I have never had a bratwurst, but I do this out of my respect for him. I draw the line, however, at the nachos.

5. Chicago Stadium. A very nice, unassuming dog surprising in both its texture and its clarity. And so elegantly served. I've also felt the wine list is highly underrated.

And lastly, since I am feeling particularly generous, I have decided to award a bonus list. Here, then, is my . . .

BEST STADIUM FOOD, GENERALLY SPEAKING

(This category does not include private clubs or press boxes or luxury boxes or other elitist stuff. This is food any Joe Six-Pack can walk up to a stand and purchase.)

1. Chicago Stadium. Receives my rarely given "To Die For" rating. They have roast-beef sandwiches so good they would make a vegetarian kick over his juicer.

2. The Spectrum in Philadelphia. Very diverse choices. Their cheese-steak sandwiches are so good I once considered applying for the 76ers play-by-play job.

3. The old Comiskey Park, Chicago (awarded posthumously). For their League of Nations menu.

4. Montreal Forum. Ranked purely for their coffee, the strongest in sports. This coffee could keep you up three days after you're dead.

5. Capital Centre, Landover, Maryland. Very good sandwiches. Plus, for Mike Fratello, they have a children's menu.

Wait. I wasn't through. A lot of people do Marv imitations, right? But the real Albert aficionados know all the subtleties.

For instance, nobody's record is simply six and five. It's always "Six up and five down." Guys are always "looking" to do things. Nobody is shooting well, they are "On fire!" And any bad development is *"not* what he had in mind." Like some guy falls over second base: *"Not* what Tim Raines had in mind." And nobody just drops a ball or misses a shot. You are either "able" or "not able," as in "Wesley Walker . . . *not able* to hold on."

Marv has only one gear—it's a great gear, one of the greatest gears in the history of broadcasting—but there's only the one. I remember one time Marv was doing the 11 o'clock sports and, as always, he had to rush from the Knicks game at the Garden back to the studio. It was very hard for Marv to change gears that fast. So he said something like "At the Garden tonight, the Knicks were *on fire.* Here, Patrick, going glass, *able* to get inside Cartwright. Knicks win. And, on a sad note, long-time boxing official Duffy Donnagary *not able* to squeeze another day on this planet."

—Bob Costas (again)

15

The 50-Yard Chair Throw and Other Olympic Events

In the last two Summer Olympic Games, I have called riots in boxing rings and massacres on basketball courts. Maybe I should try ice skating.

The basketball, of course, was the United States men's Olympic basketball team—eleven multimillionaires and one future multimillionaire, known collectively as the Dream Team. The question was not whether they would win the gold medal at the Barcelona Olympics; the question was could there possibly be enough basketballs on the court for that many egos, not to mention enough luxury suites, enough courtesy cars and enough dinner reservations?

But the cynics were wrong. The Dream Team played exceptionally well together. In fact, they could be accused of passing *too much*. The gorgeous no-look, behind-the-back pass outshone the monster glass-threatening dunk. The Americans stir-fried every opponent they played, which, when you consider that international basketball has improved tenfold over the last five years, is brain-rattling. Unfortunately, international basketball still was one-hundredfold behind this unprecedented collection of talent. After the first game of the Tournament of the Americas in Portland, the qualifying tournament for Barcelona, you knew it. The United States whipped Cuba by 73 points. I don't know what got into the players that afternoon. Maybe it was the sight of finally seeing these beasts they'd battled all those years suddenly in the same uniform color as their own, but they were sky-high for that first game. Larry Bird, whose back was ticking toward warranty expiration, was playing defense and rebounding. Michael Jordan was combing the floor for loose balls. John Stockton, who would later break a leg, was healthy and his remarkable self. Magic Johnson was nearly as good as ever and, of course, Charles Barkley and Karl Malone—two of the most explosive finishers in the game's history—were doing some monster lane-filling.

But after that game, the players never quite achieved that state of basketball nirvana. How could they? The whole Dream Team experience was a little less like rugged international battle than a string of complicated photo opportunities. How often does the team you're about to "go to war" with ask for a picture with you before the game? With the Dream Team it happened nearly every game. I figured that the first team that came out and didn't ask for a picture would think they actually had a chance to win. That didn't happen until they faced probably the strongest international team, Croatia, led by the late New Jersey Nets star Drazen Petrovic, midway through the Barcelona Games. Not that it mattered. They *had* no chance to win.

It bordered on the surreal. In one game in Monte Carlo against the French national team, a warm-up just before the Games, Jordan was agitated with one of the French players and was letting him know it. Jordan is a bit of a trash-talker on the court anyway, but on this night he was letting this poor *homme* have it with both sides of his mouth. Jordan was cursing him out and saying things like "Did you like that move? Wanna see that one again?" Jordan spit him out like bad quiche. But when the game ended, with the United States winning by some ridiculous 40-

point margin, the French guy put his arm around Jordan and wanted a picture. Jordan was just *abusing* the guy one minute before and suddenly, a minute later, the guy wanted to be best buddies. The man's idea, I guess, was that if you are going to be humiliated, you should be humiliated by the best. Then again, maybe he just didn't speak English.

I would not say Michael Jordan was totally immersed in the entire Olympic experience. He was a little wishy-washy about going in the first place, and I personally felt that most of the time he was a little bored with the competition, like amusing your little brother with a game of chess. Besides, it was such an odd mix. Were these teams foes or fans? And if they were foes, how come he was always being told to move in closer and say cheese next to them? There was, for instance, a player on the Brazilian team at the Tournament of the Americas named Marcel Sousa who wanted only one thing out of the whole experience—to meet his idol, Bird. So Bird had some old copies of his autobiography dug up and sent to him and he signed one to Sousa. Remember, it was Brazil that handed a team of U.S. college players a stunning loss in Indianapolis in the 1987 Pan Am Games. So Bird signed his gift like this: "Too bad I wasn't in Indianapolis. I would've *killed* you." *Your pal, Larry Bird.*

And yet, at the same time, Sousa was the one—the only one—who dared taunt the Americans. Basically, he said the Americans weren't taking the tournament seriously, playing golf and hanging around with their kids and such. "It's like a vacation to them," he said. He even said Scottie Pippen had a "tan." (A tan?) "When we play them," Sousa said. "We want them at their very best."

Well, (a) this was like going up to Mike Tyson and making fun of his dental work and (b) even though the Americans *were* treating it like a vacation, they didn't want to let the whole world know. Thus, the United States had a target. They wanted to beat Brazil by 100 points, much more if possible. Here was a team with twelve NBA championship rings among them. They might have beaten them by 200. Unfortunately, Brazil never made it through the tournament and never played the United States.

Barkley told me later he thought Brazil tanked just to avoid them. Sounds like a smart move.

Still, the whole deal was such an obvious mismatch that the players needed *something* to get motivated, even if the something was pretty lame. For instance: In Barcelona, the players suddenly got incensed because there had been a couple of articles criticizing them for not staying in the Olympic Village with the rest of the athletes. Of course, that was preposterous. Anybody who saw the players get mobbed in the Opening Ceremonies—especially Magic Johnson—knew that the athletes wouldn't have had two seconds' sleep in the Olympic Village. And if the other athletes didn't get them, their legs and arms hanging over the edges of six-foot beds would have. Besides, precious few of the pro athletes in the games—the tennis players, for instance—stayed in the Village. One, Jim Courier, tried but lasted only two nights before the lack of air conditioning, privacy and sleep drove him back to his $800-a-night hotel.

It mattered not a whit that only two or three writers had written it and that it was obviously unfounded, the players acted like somebody had set fire to their lawn. "If you don't like our hotel, screw you," was the general posture taken. "It's us against the world."

Charles Barkley was the ringleader of that movement and it's not surprising. Barkley, like Jordan, is the kind of athlete who, to play at all, needs some kind of war to enlist in. Magic could get psyched up for a game against the NBC pages, but not Barkley. Thus, he took a little bump from an Angolan player—an *Angolan!*—as a personal insult and threw an elbow at the poor man's thorax. Barkley became the Villain of Barcelona and relished the boos that would rain down upon him at the Olympic basketball arena in the tiny village of Badalona, fifteen minutes from Barcelona. What's ironic is that Barkley was the *one* Dream Teamer who seemed to be loving Barcelona. Every day, even game days, Barkley would play golf, sometimes 36 holes in a day. And every night, Barkley would stroll down the boulevard known as Las Ramblas, the human cavalcade of people and music and bars and restaurants and street-crossing waiters in the city's center. You always knew it was Barkley by the river of people following him. It was a peculiar sight. He went without protection, even though he was a member of a team that would leave their hotel for games with police escorts front and back and two helicopters overhead. Barkley didn't care. He laughed and joked and talked and walked with the multitudes who followed him. To the untrained eye, he must have looked like a very tall, black Pied Piper.

Jordan, though, and many of the others chose to stay in, near the air conditioning and the endless card games, usually with his buddy, Ahmad Rashad. Most of the players had their families with them and the hotel set up playrooms for their kids and American meals for their stomachs. Still, there were times—even during games—when the players seemed bored as sixth-graders diagramming sentences. One time, for instance, the Americans were whitewashing Germany, which was playing this tiny little point guard who looked like he was about 40. Bird walked over near our table, making sure we could hear him, and hollered to his teammates, "I got Fratello."

Ironically, the greatest basketball the Dream Team played— maybe the greatest basketball of all time—was played in front of exactly nobody.

It was a scrimmage in Monaco before the Games began. The players were growing tired of beating up on French Foreign Legion teams and the boys from the Monte Carlo Y, so Olympic coach Chuck Daly finally let them go after each other, one time. It happened in a tiny little gym in France. The people who were there say it was basketball played at the highest level ever. No reporters were allowed in. No cameras either, though some snuck in for moments at a time. It was Jordan's team vs. Magic's, six on a squad, and each six could make a case as the best six players on the planet were it not for the other six.

They say Jordan proved himself to be twice as good as any other player on the court. Whether that's true or not, I think Jordan may have had a little motivation. Despite statements over the years to the contrary, there has always been a little professional jealousy between he and Magic. There was Magic's friendship with Isiah, who, for years, was Jordan's sworn enemy. And

177

then, at a banquet a few nights before that scrimmage, Magic stood up in front of a room of people that included Prince Albert and Prince Rainier and said, "It's nice to spend this time with royalty. Although we *have* been spending time with God," and looked kiddingly at Jordan. Basketball-wise, he might have been right.

Besides playing his own teammates, the only other factor that seemed to get Jordan especially motivated were the words "Toni Kukoc," Croatia's star guard. Two years before, the Bulls general manager, Jerry Krause, in fact, was trying to sign Kukoc. Kukoc was in the Italian pro leagues and was drafted as a future by Krause. The problem was, as Krause was trying to sign Kukoc, he hadn't quite sealed up Scottie Pippen's contract, mostly because of the team's complicated salary-cap structure. That angered Jordan. Jordan would tell me, off-camera, that the players didn't want Kukoc unless Pippen was taken care of first. Besides, they'd been winning and winning big with the players they had. "You go with who got you this far," Jordan would say. I'd say it on the air. Kukoc was getting our NBC games in Italy and would call Krause up and say, "I'm not sure I should come. The players don't want me."

"Where did you hear that?" Krause would say.

"On TV," he'd say.

So Krause came to me about it, livid. "Why are you saying that the players don't want Kukoc?"

"I'm getting it straight from Scottie Pippen and Michael Jordan," I'd say.

"They're ballplayers," he said. "They have a different agenda."

"Well, that may be. But they still don't want him."

Krause was quoted in the book *Jordan Rules,* by Sam Smith, as telling Bulls coach Phil Jackson that he'd see that I'd never work again. Krause even asked Jordan to call Kukoc and tell him the players really *did* want him. Jordan refused. Pippen refused. Krause finally got center Bill Cartwright to do it. Cartwright is a wonderful guy, but it probably didn't mean a whole hill of beans to Kukoc, who eventually decided not to sign. (Later, in 1993, he did.)

Anyway, when the Americans took on Croatia, Jordan was pumped up to shut Kukoc down as a little message to Krause. And so he did, along with Pippen. They hounded that poor man the entire night, holding him to four points and about six deep breaths. He was lucky to get out still wearing his uniform. They stripped him of everything else, including his dreams of eventual NBA glory. Afterward, Jordan said he didn't know if Kukoc was quite ready for the NBA. No, I think Kukoc is ready for the NBA. He's a terrific, unselfish player. In fact, when the Americans played Croatia again, in the final, Kukoc comported himself very well. What Kukoc is not ready for is trying to play a game with two of the league's best defenders on him all night.

Mostly, the Olympics for these guys were a chance to goof off, get to know each other and, for two hours a night, beat the spleens out of the basketball-playing world. What surprised the Dream Team members, I think, was what fun they had. Bird (Larry) and Patrick Ewing (Bird called him "Harry") formed an unlikely friendship. They each seemed to delight in devastating the other one. I sat with them one night and Larry seemed to be getting the best of "Harry." Bird could run off, verbatim, the play-by-play of every game the two had played together. He particularly liked to recall an exhibition game when 7–2 Yugoslav Stojko Vrankovic, a pure twelfth-man stiff, blocked three of Ewing's shots. To salt the wound, every ten minutes or so he'd ask Ewing how many championship rings he had. Zero. Bird? Three.

There were enough mental snapshots that I've kept from that one week in Monaco to last a lifetime. Like the time a French reporter asked Barkley a question in French. When he was done, Barkley's eyebrows raised a couple inches and he said, "What'd you just say about my mama?"

Like the guy who was gazing at the players standing in front of their swank Monte Carlo hotel and drove his Mercedes right through the plate-glass window of a jewelry store.

Like the time the Americans played the French nationals in an exhibition game and Prince Rainier wanted to sit with someone who really understood the game. "Fine," said a USA Basketball official. "Who would you like?"

I'd Love to But I Have a Game

"Chuck Daly," said the Prince.

Apparently, it took a little while to convince the Prince that Coach Daly might be a little busy during the game. It evened out, though. The players asked if Princess Stephanie could sit on the bench during the time-outs.

There was the public-address announcer for that game, who took a hand-held mike with him out on the floor and started making like Tony Bennett during the introduction of the rosters. It was "And now, one of my very dear friends, one of my favorite players . . ." Then, after every basket, he would say, *"Ouiiiii!"* I gave him a strong 7.

The Americans waltzed away with the gold. Their blowouts became commonplace and, to some, dull. What they were doing was so phenomenal that it began to look easy. This wasn't Oregon State they were playing. Had the United States sent a team of collegians, I think the chances are very good that they could have lost to Croatia or Lithuania. As it was, the Americans won by a colossal 43.75 points per game. If that record is ever broken, I'll eat my Kobi tie.

As for suspenseful moments, there were only two. One was how my color analyst, Señor Fratello, was going to get out of his on-air statement he made about the Spanish star "Eppy," who wasn't getting much playing time because he was much older than most of the players. "Hey, he's getting older with each passing year," Mike said. I think this is the kind of incisive international commentary NBC has been lacking.

The other was what some of the players who represent Nike were going to do for the gold medal award ceremony, for which they were required to wear the warm-up suits provided by Reebok, one of USA Basketball's official suppliers. A man signed to Nike would rather dip himself in tuna and swim naked through a tank of sharks than wear a Reebok logo. Jordan had warned he might not even show up if he had to wear the suit. Eventually, he and Barkley and Pippen and a few others wore American flags draped across the jacket's insignia. I said on the air, "Michael Jordan has wrapped himself in the red, white and blue—and *not* for patriotic reasons."

The 50-Yard Chair Throw and Other Olympic Events

But any controversy that stemmed from the Dream Team was nothing compared to what we went through covering the 1988 Seoul Olympics boxing with my analyst Ferdie (the Fight Doctor) Pacheco. That Olympics, one rule basically applied: Anything that could go wrong, did.

It started innocently enough. A few technicians with NBC decided to have T-shirts drawn up with two boxers superimposed over the Korean flag. Innocent enough, right? Well, in Korea, it is a serious show of disrespect to put anything over the Korean flag. When the design started going around the compounds, we had more than a few Koreans upset. The more the executives tried to explain, the worse it got.

Then we got a load of the boxing setup, your basic Two-Ring Circus. There were so many fights that they needed two boxing rings to get them all in. The boxers in one ring were to listen for a bell; the boxers in the other for a tone. Naturally, it didn't work. A boxer in the bell ring would react to the tone 50 yards away and stop fighting, thus earning a right cross for his trouble. The boxer in the tone ring would fight when he heard a bell. It was chaos.

We said as much, and the Koreans, who were seeing our NBC feed over Armed Forces Television, were not happy with our objectivity. Apparently, in Korea one does not say disparaging things about a local fighter, a local fight or a local fight tournament and we had done them all. We both received death threats. The only difference was, Ferdie's were from NBC executives.

And finally came the fight between a Korean named Bjun Jong-il and a Hungarian named Alexander Hristov. As the fight wore on, Hristov began doing a curious thing. In clinches, he would put a bear hug around the shorter Bjun and lift him, causing the Korean's head to bang into Hristov's chin. The referee, a New Zealander named Keith Walker, took these as head butts by the Korean and assessed him a penalty point, not once, but twice.

With the help of the points, the Hungarian won by decision, causing loud whistling in the arena. Suddenly a chair was tossed into the ring over our heads and then more chairs. Incredibly, it was the yellow-jacketed Korean security guards throwing the chairs. I can't believe that was in their job description. Then, when Bjun's manager took a swing at Walker, all hell broke loose. Some of the security guards were trying to get through other security guards to get to Walker. Save us from our protectors. I really wasn't sure he was going to get out alive. Come to think of it, I wasn't sure Ferdie and I were going to get out alive either.

We had not been on the air live at the time but soon enough we received word that NBC's Olympic host, Bryant Gumbel, was about to go to us live. Moments before he did, the lights went out. The same thought must have passed between Ferdie and me: the death threats. The crowd was still very much there, only now we couldn't see them. I was somewhat unnerved, and it didn't help to hear Ferdie nervously whisper, quite seriously, "Well, Marv, it's been a nice run. But I think it's all over for us now. Fortunately my wife and my family are in good shape financially."

We found out later they turned out the lights only to dissuade others from joining in the riot. I'm not sure I understand that logic. Personally, I think it works just the opposite. To the average potential rioter, you turn out the lights and it's like, "Look, the lights are out. Nobody can see us. Let's go drop a table on Marv's head."

Finally, the riot was quelled and the lights were turned back on. Afterwards, our fearless sideline reporter, New York *Newsday*'s Wally Matthews, tried to interview the security guard who threw the chair. The guard insisted he didn't speak English. That was odd, since my son Kenny, who was in Seoul as our researcher, had traded Olympic pins with him earlier in the day and was vigorously negotiating with him in English.

Then, as Lewis Carroll once wrote, things got "curiouser and curiouser." The defeated fighter, Bjun, refused to leave the ring. Would not go. He staged a sit-in. Nobody could get him to leave. He sat there for 10 minutes, 20 minutes, 30 minutes. Finally, at 42 minutes, we had a bit of activity. He got a chair.

There is not a lot of scintillating play-by-play you can do about a man sitting in a chair. *There it is! He's changed elbows!* At last, after 51 minutes, he left. At 52 minutes, so did we.

But there's an interesting sidenote to that remarkable night that few people know:

Bjun Jong-il is now godfather to my children.

I have seen mistakes made of every kind, color and stripe. I once interviewed a San Francisco 49er who said that the team just needed to get "mo-modem" back on their side.

"You mean mo-MENT-um," I corrected.

"Right," he said. "Mo-modem."

I have heard athletes say after losing an important game that they now had their "backs to the driver's seat."

I myself once stood next to the trainer of the New Jersey Nets and not remembered his name for the life of me. To make it worse, as I was stammering for his name, I said, on network television, "I can't believe I can't remember his name. And he's my best friend!" Which was interesting, since I'd met him for the first time that day.

But the mistake I got the most satisfaction from was made by Marv himself. He was broadcasting a 1993 Indiana Pacers–New York Knicks playoff game one night when they showed former USC basketball star Cheryl Miller sitting in the stands.

"There's Reggie Miller's brother," Marv said on the air.

"Are you sure that's what you mean?" asked his color man, John Andariese.

"Of course I'm sure," said Marv.

So, either Marv has been wearing headphones too long or he missed some very important health classes in junior high.

—Ahmad Rashad

16

Good Night, Kenny

I would get seriously hurt at this point if I didn't let you know, here at the end, that I really *do* have a life. I have four terrific kids. There's the twins, Denise and Brian, both of whom I am convinced will run a good percentage of the world someday. There's my older daughter, Jackie, who despite her surroundings never could stand sports. Can you imagine what dinner-table conversation was like at our house for somebody who wasn't interested in sports? Brian was at one time planning to be Commissioner of the NHL. Now his focus is on politics. Denise knows more professional athletes by face than some general managers. My ex-wife, Benita, never missed a game. So, for Jackie, there was no avoiding it. Though she'd never want to admit it, just by osmosis she knows more about sports than most bartenders. Every once in a while, she'll be watching television or something and we'll be talking sports and she'll just blurt out, "The Cubs had their chance in 1969. Kessinger choked at the plate."

And, of course, I have my older son, Kenny, who is entering

his second season as one of the television voices of the Washington Capitals of the National Hockey League. Soon there will be an Albert broadcasting the games of *every single sports franchise in the country!*

It's scary how much Kenny was like me as a kid. He would do anything to get on the air. One time, a tiny-voiced kid called my talk show and said, "What do you think about Willis Reed?" Well, I tried to discourage little kids from calling the show because you often get a nowhere question that slowed down the pace, so I sort of jumped on this kid. "Well, what about him? What specifically about Willis would you like to know?"

There was a long pause. Finally, the voice said, "Dad? It's Kenny."

Naturally, I hung up on him.

Kenny's been sitting at my side at games since he was five years old, keeping his own private stat sheet. When he got old enough, I actually did make him my stat man for most games. It was Kenny, by the way, who gave Phil Jackson the nickname "Action" when he was with the Knicks. Kenny was playing with this toy by the same name and so I started calling Phil that. Come to think of it, Kenny still plays with that toy.

Sportscasting was in his genes. He was born during a Rangers road trip, the son of a Knicks sportscaster and an ex-Mets usherette. Most nights, the closest Kenny got to a bedtime story from me was a power-play goal off the post in the second period. Harry Caray used to stop his broadcasts of the St. Louis Cardinals games at exactly 8:30 and say, "Good night, Skip." Steve Wulf of *Sports Illustrated* asked Skip about it once and Skip remembered it well. In fact, he said it became something of an embarrassment after a while, especially when he was playing football at Webster Groves High School outside St. Louis. "Just before the snap," Skip said, "the big guy across the line from me would snarl and say, 'Good night, Skip.' "

Kenny was as obsessed with it as a kid as I had been. He had his own non-air radio station, WKGA—Kenneth Gary Albert—and whenever a sports personality would come over to the house, Kenny would hold him hostage and do interviews for WKGA

186

into his tape deck, sometimes in the bathroom. I mean, *what kind of kid would do that?* As he got older, he did high school games on tape at Schreiber High School in Port Washington, New York. Like his Uncle Al, Kenny played college hockey and then would report on it for the college station. He also broadcast the NYU basketball games on WNYU, the school station. Once, as a guest announcer, I did the first half with him. I did play-by-play and he did color. It was a great thrill, though I thought he got a little short with me afterwards when I asked for the appropriate fee.

Pretty soon he was doing reports on WFAN all-sports radio in New York and subbing on New York Islanders hockey radio broadcasts. I remember that one of his first Islanders games was against the Rangers. I saw him beforehand and I said, "Hey, we *really* need a stat guy tonight, whaddya say?" He did not seem amused.

It was a little hard for me to picture Kenny doing the Islanders. Kenny grew up intensely disliking the Islanders. When the Islanders played the Soviets, Kenny rooted for the Soviets. Now he was the substitute voice of the Islanders? In fact, his color man for those games was Bob Nystrom, the rough-and-tumble ex-Islander. Kenny used to *despise* him. I suggested to Nystrom that, while on the air, he pull Kenny's shirt over his head and beat him up.

One thing, though, Kenny knows his stuff. One night, there was a stop in play and the clock read 7:11. "Hey, Bob," Kenny said. "Does seven-eleven mean anything to you?" Nystrom knew immediately what he meant and smiled. Nystrom scored the goal that gave the Islanders their first Stanley Cup in 1980, at 7:11 of overtime.

Finally, after working two seasons doing play-by-play for the minor league Baltimore Skipjacks, Kenny, age 24, got the call from the Capitals. I'll never forget that first night the Rangers played the Capitals. To see him calling the same NHL game I was calling and knowing that he had made it gave me chills.

I was so proud. Afterwards I said, "Whaddya say tomorrow night we go out and have a big celebration dinner?"

"Gee, Dad," he said, "I'd love to but I have a game."

$16^1/_2$

Overtime

Sorry, but the 1993 NBA playoffs and finals were too wonderful to slip by without a mention. No, not because of the monster finals between Michael Jordan's Chicago Bulls and Charles Barkley's Phoenix Suns. And not because of the classic semifinal series the Bulls waged with the New York Knicks. And not because of the incredible ratings NBC received (best in NBA history). No, I will always remember the 1993 playoffs because Mike (the Czar of the TeleStrator) Fratello took the Cleveland Cavaliers head coaching job and became, quite simply, the Czar of Cleveland.

We'd been hearing that rumor for a week before it happened. We'd pass him messages just before the start of crucial games that would read, "What would you do with Bobby Phills?" Or, "How about trading Jay Gidinger for Scott Hastings?" For some reason, Mike would always crumple these missives up. We fretted how Mike could go to Cleveland when every time he'd broadcast a Cleveland game, he'd constantly mispronounced the name of forward Mike Sanders. He'd always say *"Saunders,"* which is the name of the Knicks trainer, Mike Saunders. So what's the first thing he does when he gets the job? He drafts Chris Mills, who will replace Sanders in the starting lineup. The man is *cold.*

Besides Fratello actually being allowed back into the NBA, the biggest surprise of the playoffs was what happened to the Knicks. They changed. They spent the first half of the regular season as the Bullies of Broadway, menacing opponents, knocking them down, stealing their lunch money. It had seemed out of character for a Pat Riley–coached team, until Magic Johnson corrected us. He told us, on the air, that Riley used to have a rule on those L.A. Lakers teams: Any player who allowed an opponent to come through the lane for a lay-up without getting fouled hard and/or knocked down was fined. And any player who helped an opponent up was also fined. But all that changed when they went to Phoenix in March and engaged in a game of basketbrawl. Featuring a main event of the Suns' Kevin Johnson and the Knicks' Doc Rivers, the fight card that night set NBA records for the most ejections and fines in one game, including a huge one against Knicks guard Greg Anthony, who wasn't even in *uniform.*

After that, the Knicks were never quite the same. They were so roundly criticized by the press and so gun-shy of the league office that they became squeamish. They lost that deep-down Charles Bronson orneriness. When Chicago faced them in the semifinals, the Bulls were able to play without each of them turning into a human welt, and they won in six.

Sportsmanship and friendship came up a lot during these playoffs. Magic insisted over and over again that in the playoffs, you cannot be friends with your opponents if you expect to win. He even said that his friendship with Isiah Thomas changed the year they went head-to-head in the finals. He pointed out that what Michael Jordan was doing by having dinner with Barkley at his Chicago restaurant during the finals would pay off only for Michael. When you look back on it, he was right. Barkley never *once* knocked Jordan down. Not to say this was the only reason the Bulls won in six—but I felt it was a factor.

Funny, much the same thing was said about Knick Charles Oakley's friendship with Jordan. Oakley never once dealt with Jordan aggressively in their series, either. Dale Carnegie would have made a nice career in this league.

Not everything went smoothly for Jordan in the playoffs. The night between Games 1 and 2 of the Knicks series, both won by the Knicks, Jordan was seen gambling as late as 2:30 A.M. in an Atlantic City casino, according to the New York *Times*. Then, during the same week, a San Diego businessman named Richard Esquinas claimed that Jordan lost $1.25 million to him playing golf in 1991. Jordan denied that figure and also denied he had a gambling problem. I certainly don't know if he has one or not. But I know one thing: The same obsession that makes Michael Jordan the most viciously competitive and unstoppable player in NBA history on the court does not get left in his locker when he leaves the court. He is what he is. If Jordan lost one hundred Dr Peppers to you in a game of Ping-Pong, he would ring your doorbell and call you and bother you and harass you until you gave him another chance to beat you. This is a man who once walked off a practice court during a scrimmage because he thought his coach, Doug Collins, had the score wrong. If he is addicted to anything, it's winning. You could no more ask him to change that part of his character than you could get a zebra to change the color of his stripes.

There were three incredible games in those finals, starting with the Suns' triple-overtime win in Game 3 in Chicago when they absolutely, positively had to win, down 0–2. That game broke all kinds of ratings records, and even though Bulls coach Phil Jackson said it wasn't a classic because so few points were scored in the first two overtimes, I disagree. That's *exactly* what made it fascinating: playing on only one day's rest, great players at that level sagging under the enormity of the pressure. Phoenix eventually hung tough and won in the grittiest snake pit in basketball.

Game 5 was unforgettable, too, in that everybody and their sister were picking Chicago to close it out that night, including the Chicago police. They feared rioting should the Bulls win. It was eerie driving to Chicago Stadium that night. Windows were boarded up. A phalanx of policemen holding guns guarded the upscale department stores on Michigan Avenue. It was like London waiting to be bombed. But Barkley, playing with only one good arm, changed everybody's plans with a magnificent game and the Suns pulled off one of the great upsets in finals history, taking two out of three in Chicago. When it was over, Barkley said, "Take down the plywood, Chicago. There won't be no riots tonight."

No, unfortunately, the riot would come two nights later, after Game 6, when the Bulls' John Paxson made one of the most thrilling bombs in NBA history. With 6 seconds left and the Bulls trailing by 2, Horace Grant, who had lost his shooting nerve, gave up a 5-footer and peeled a pass outside to Paxson, waiting at the 3-point line. There wasn't a Sun anywhere near him. As Paxson squared up to shoot, you realized he held the 1993 NBA title in his hands. If he made it, the Bulls would make history as the first three-time defending champions since the advent of free agency. If he missed it, the series would be tied, Phoenix would have all the momentum, and the Suns would most certainly take Game 7. Looking back on all my years in basketball, I can't remember a title riding on one basketball shot.

The call was simple. "Paxson . . . Yesssss!"

The hero was, nonetheless, Jordan, who averaged more points during a final series than any player in history. He was the finals MVP for the third straight year. By virtue of sheer boredom, though, the writers voted Barkley the regular season MVP, and I was glad for him, but of course there is nobody to compare with Jordan. You give it to somebody else once in a while just to give the engraver a change of pace. They might just as easily have given it to the Knicks' Patrick Ewing, too, who carried his team to 60 regular season victories, but Ewing will never win awards like that as long as he chooses to remain such a private person. Barkley is charming: During our pre-game opening before Game 5, Barkley actually got out of the lay-up line and stuck his head between Magic and me while we were on the air. "Just seein' if you guys were picking us tonight," he said. (To which I replied, "Charles, we're *very* busy.") That's the kind of stuff that makes

191

you like him. Jordan, too, is incredibly cooperative. But Ewing, though very bright, chooses to be the NBA's version of Greta Garbo. He "vants to be alone." It's not fair, of course—he should be judged purely on his basketball. But these are human beings voting and if you step on a guy's toe enough times, he does not much feel like showering you with orchids.

By 7 A.M. the day after the finals, the Czar was already in Ohio, his head buried in films. I needed to ask him something so I called him up.

"Hey, Mike, how you doing?" I asked.

There was a long pause on the other end. Then a sigh.

"Marv," he said at last. "I *told* you. The relationship is over."